中华民族的
图腾

中国八千年龙文化文物精品

LOONG
THE TOTEM OF THE CHINESE NATION

EXQUISITE CULTURAL RELICS OF
CHINA'S 8000 YEARS LOONG CULTURE

中国历史研究院
编

社会科学文献出版社
SOCIAL SCIENCES ACADEMIC PRESS (CHINA)

主办单位

中国历史研究院

承办单位

中国历史研究院考古研究所　中国考古博物馆

展览日期

2024 年 4 月 29 日—12 月 31 日

协办单位

内蒙古博物院

内蒙古自治区文物考古研究院

巴林右旗博物馆

林西博物馆

翁牛特旗博物馆

敖汉博物馆

辽宁省文物考古研究院

徐州博物馆

扬州市文物考古研究所

浙江省文物考古研究所

安徽博物院

安徽省文物考古研究所

蚌埠市博物馆

含山博物馆

泉州市文物保护中心

郑州市文物考古研究院

殷墟博物馆

荆州博物馆

四川省文物考古研究院

四川广汉三星堆博物馆

罗平县文物局

陕西历史博物馆

青海省文物考古研究院

目 录

前　言

在 2024 年春节团拜会上，习近平总书记深刻指出："龙是中华民族的图腾，具有刚健威武的雄姿、勇猛无畏的气概、福泽四海的情怀、强大无比的力量，既象征着五千年来中华民族自强不息、奋斗进取的精神血脉，更承载着新时代新征程亿万中华儿女推进强国建设、民族复兴伟业的坚定意志和美好愿望。甲辰龙年，希望全国人民振奋龙马精神，以龙腾虎跃、鱼跃龙门的干劲闯劲，开拓创新、拼搏奉献，共同书写中国式现代化建设新篇章。"习近平总书记的重要讲话不仅彰显了龙在中华文明发展史中的重要地位和时代价值，更为我们在新时代传承和弘扬中华优秀传统文化指明了方向。

党的二十届三中全会提出，要"构建中华文明标识体系"。龙文化，作为璀璨的中华文明瑰宝，贯穿了中华民族的历史长河。龙，见证了历史的波澜壮阔、民族的交汇融合，以及一代代中华儿女的进取奋斗，它是中华民族独特精神标识的重要组成部分。习近平总书记强调："文化没有断过流、始终传承下来的只有中国。我们这些人也延续着黑头发、黄皮肤，我们叫龙的传人。"这充分体现了龙文化所蕴含的中华民族文化根脉和精神传承。作为龙的传人，我们肩负着传承和弘扬龙文化的历史使命，要深刻理解龙所代表的源远流长、博大精深的中华文明，感知中华民族的伟大精神和优秀传统，从而坚定文化自信，这是我们在新时代坚守中华文化立场、推进文化强国建设的重要基础。

在中国浩如烟海的文献典籍中，大量关于龙的文字记述为我们研究龙文化提供了丰富的历史资料。《诗经·商颂·玄鸟》记载："天命玄鸟，降而生商。……龙旂十乘，大糦是承。"《礼记·礼器》有云："礼有以文为贵者，天子龙衮。"龙自出现以来就与礼仪、礼制密切相关，是中华民族的图腾和重要精神符号。

考古发掘出土的各类龙文物，则以实物的形式，让我们对龙的文化内涵有了更深刻、更直观的认识，真切感受到中华文明与龙的内在紧密关联。2024 甲辰龙年，在中国社会科学院党组、中国历史研究院党委的统一部署和高翔院长的直接领导下，中国考古博物馆联合 23 家考古文博单位，举办"龙·中华民族的图腾——中国八千年龙文化精品文物展"，这一展览以考古实证阐释古代中国龙形象、内涵的演变，具有重要的文化意义。

本次展览呈现出三个显著特点。其一，展品的选择精益求精。在中国考古博物馆现有馆藏的基础上，精心挑选110余件龙文物，其年代跨度从距今约8000年的新石器时代中期直至明清，涵盖了红山文化的玉"C"形龙、玉猪龙，凌家滩文化的玉龙首形器，良渚文化的玉龙首镯，陶寺文化的陶彩绘龙纹盘，新砦文化的龙纹陶片，二里头文化的鱼龙纹陶盆，商代殷墟遗址出土的铜龙纹盘、三星堆遗址出土的铜猪鼻龙形器，西周张家坡墓地出土的玉龙凤人物形佩饰等众多优中选优的精品文物。这些文物犹如一部部生动的史书，向我们诉说着龙文化在不同历史时期的发展与演变。其二，展览强调二重证据法的应用。在中国最早的成熟文字甲骨文中就已出现"龙"字，《诗经》《史记》《说文解字》等文献中也有诸多关于龙形象的记载与解读。展览通过"纸上之材料"与"地下之新材料"的相互印证，展现了中国龙文化的悠久历史，体现了现代历史学研究方法在文化传承中的重要作用。其三，展览注重将传统文化与现代科技相结合。利用投影、智慧屏介绍考古发掘历程，向观众多角度展示龙文物细部特征，让观众能够更加直观地体验现代科技为传统文化传播带来的便利。这也是推动中华优秀传统文化创造性转化、创新性发展的有益尝试。

　　一部龙文化史就是一部浓缩的中华文化发展史，更充分体现了中华文明突出的连续性、创新性、统一性、包容性、和平性。龙出东方，从新石器时代满天星斗的各地原始文化中以图腾的形式孕育而生，随着多元一体的重瓣花朵式史前社会发展而融汇创新；龙行天下，在中原广域王权国家形成和发展过程中逐渐成形，成为中华文明中最重要的文化基因；龙泽四海，其形象及精神实质自秦汉一统一直延续至今，充满了"日日新"的勃勃生机，展现了中华文明强大的生命力和凝聚力。

　　"天行健，君子以自强不息。"中华文明及其精神标识紧密关联着当下与未来，既是中国特色社会主义道路的历史根基，也是我们建设中华民族现代文明的文化底色，更是我们在世界文化激荡中站稳脚跟的力量源泉。中国龙文化之所以能够如此长盛不衰并具有历久弥新的生命力，正是得益于不同时代文化的滋养，以及一代代中国人的开拓与创新。面向未来，我们要深入贯彻习近平文化思想，以龙文化为载体，进一步激发全民族文化创新创造活力，让龙文化这一中华文明的精神标识在社会主义新时代焕发出更加耀眼的光芒，为实现中华民族伟大复兴的中国梦凝聚强大的精神动力，谱写绚丽篇章。

刘国祥

2025 年 1 月 5 日

Preface

President Xi Jinping pointed out in his important speech at the Spring Festival reception in 2024 that as the totem of the Chinese nation, loong is deemed strong, fearless, benevolent and powerful, and it not only embodies the Chinese nation's spirit of ceaselessly pursuing self-improvement, hard work and enterprise for 5,000 years, but also encapsulates the determination and aspiration of hundreds of millions of Chinese people to build China into a strong country and realize national rejuvenation. In the upcoming Year of the Loong, we hope that people across the country embrace a spirit of vitality and determination as represented by the loong. With great momentum and ambition, we will explore new ground with hard work and dedication, collectively writing a new chapter in advancing Chinese modernization. The speech of President Xi Jinping not only highlights the significant position of loong culture in the spiritual inheritance of the Chinese nation, but also gives the direction for us to inherit and carry forward the excellent traditional Chinese culture in the new era.

The third plenary session of the 20th Central Committee of the Communist Party of China advocates to build a system of Chinese cultural identity symbols. Loong culture, as a brilliant treasure of Chinese civilization, has occurred throughout the history of the Chinese nation. The loong has witnessed the magnificent history, the convergence and fusion of nationalities, and the enterprising struggles of generations of Chinese people, and it has become an essential part of the unique spiritual identity of the Chinese nation. President Xi Jinping emphatically stated that "Chinese civilization is a unique lasting culture in the world that passed down through generations consistently. Black hair and yellow skin, we call ourselves descendants of the loong." This fully embodies the Chinese nation's cultural roots and spiritual inheritance contained in loong culture. As the loong's heirs, we undertake the historical mission of carrying forward the loong culture. We should deeply understand the long history and profound Chinese civilization represented by the loong and perceive the great spirit and excellent traditions of the nation to strengthen our cultural self-confidence, which is an essential foundation for us to adhere to the stance of the Chinese culture and promote the construction of a strong cultural nation in the new era.

In Chinese literature, many written records about the loong provide us with rich historical information for studying the loong culture. Since its appearance in the documents, the loong has been closely related to rituals and ceremonies and is the Chinese nation's totem and crucial spiritual symbol.

The cultural relics unearthed from archaeological excavations, in the form of physical objects, allow us to have a deeper and more intuitive understanding of the cultural connotation of the loong and truly feel the intrinsic close connection between Chinese civilization and the loong. In 2024, the Year of the Loong, under the unified deployment of the Party Leadership Group of the Chinese Academy of Social Sciences, the Party Committee of the Chinese Academy of History, and led by CASS President Gao Xiang, the Chinese Archaeological Museum, in cooperation with 23 archaeological and cultural institutions, organized the "Loong-the totem of the Chinese nation-the exhibition of exquisite cultural relics of China's 8000 years loong culture". This exhibition is of great cultural significance as it explains the evolution of the image and connotation of the loong in ancient China with archaeological evidence.

The exhibition has three notable characteristics. Firstly, we carefully chose the exhibits. Based on the holding collection of the Chinese Archaeological Museum, more than 110 pieces of loong relics have been carefully selected, spanning from the middle of the Neolithic period, which is 8,000 years ago, to the end of the Qing Dynasty, including the *C*-shaped jade loong and jade coiled loong of the Hongshan culture, the jade ware in the shape of loong head of the Lingjiatan culture, the jade bracelet with loong heads design of the Liangzhu culture, the painted pottery plate with loong design of the Taosi culture, the incised pottery lid sherd of the Xinzhai culture, the pottery basin with fish and loong design of the Erlitou culture, the bronze plate with loong design unearthed from ruins of Yin of the Shang Dynasty, the loong-shaped bronze ware unearthed from Sanxingdui site, and the jade pendant with loong, phoenix and human design unearthed from Zhangjiapo cemetery of the Western Zhou Dynasty. These splendid relics are like vivid history books, showing the development and evolution of the loong culture in different historical periods. Secondly, the exhibition focuses on the application of the double evidence method. The character "loong" already appeared in the oracle bone inscriptions, the earliest mature Chinese writing, and there are many records and interpretations of the image of the loong, such as in the *Shijing* (*Classic of Poetry*), *Shiji* (*Records of the Grand Historian*), and *Shuowen Jiezi Dictionary*. Through the archaeological relics and historical documents, the exhibition fully substantiates the long history of Chinese loong culture and reflects the critical role of modern academic research methodology of the historical discipline in cultural inheritance. Thirdly, the exhibition stresses combining traditional culture with modern technology. We use projections and multi-touch screens to introduce the archaeological excavation process and show the detailed characteristics of cultural relics from multiple angles so that the audience can more intuitively experience the convenience brought by modern science and technology. This is also a salutary attempt to promote the creative transformation and innovative development of outstanding traditional Chinese culture.

A history of the loong culture is a condensed history of the development of Chinese culture, which fully embodies the outstanding consistency, originality, unity, inclusiveness, and peaceful nature of Chinese civilization. From the primitive cultures of various places in the Neolithic Age, the loong emerged as a totem, merging and innovating with developing a diverse and integrated prehistoric society. In the formation and development of the Central Plains territorial kingship state, the image of the Chinese loong was finally formed. The loong became a crucial cultural gene in Chinese civilization. Since the unification of the Qin and Han Dynasties, the image of the loong and its spiritual essence has continued to this day, demonstrating Chinese civilization's strong vitality and cohesion.

Chinese civilization and its spiritual identity are closely related to the present and the future. They are not only the historical foundation of the road of socialism with Chinese characteristics but also the spiritual underpinning of the modern civilization of the Chinese nation, as well as the source of our cultural self-confidence in maintaining stability in the cultural turbulence of the world. The Chinese loong culture has flourished so well and has everlasting vitality because of the nourishment of culture in different eras and the pioneering and innovation of generations of Chinese people. Looking to the future, we should sincerely implement Xi Jinping Thought on Culture, take loong culture as a carrier, and further stimulate the vitality of national cultural innovation and creativity so that the loong culture, the spiritual symbol of Chinese civilization, will shine even brighter in the new era of socialism, and gather a strong spiritual impetus for the dream of achieving the great rejuvenation of the Chinese nation and write a splendid chapter.

Liu Guoxiang

January 5, 2025

概　述

考古实证中国八千年龙文化

　　龙作为中华民族独特的文化符号，其影响深远而广泛。长久以来，龙在中国人的心中有吉祥、权威、力量等多种含义。习近平总书记在甲辰龙年春节团拜会上的重要讲话中指出："龙是中华民族的图腾，具有刚健威武的雄姿、勇猛无畏的气概、福泽四海的情怀、强大无比的力量。"中国龙文化历史悠久。早在新石器时代，中华大地上就出现了众多与龙相关的遗存，随着考古工作的不断深入，越来越多的实物发现为龙文化在中华大地上的传承发展提供了鲜明的物证。对龙文化起源和发展历程的研究，有助于我们更深入地理解中华民族早期的精神世界、社会组织和文化交流。

一、距今 8000 年前后龙形象的起源

　　进入新石器时代，先民就已基于自身熟悉的动物形象创造龙的形象，体现出了独特的审美与信仰。其中，最具代表性的是兴隆洼文化遗址。兴隆洼文化是辽西地区新石器时代的重要考古学文化，其年代上限为距今约 8200 年，奠定了西辽河流域在东北地区新石器时代文化发展的核心地位。其遗址包括内蒙古敖汉旗兴隆洼及兴隆沟、克什克腾旗南台子、林西白音长汗、阜新查海等。兴隆沟遗址第一地点是兴隆洼文化中期大型聚落，在祭祀坑 H35 中发现的猪首"S"形遗迹，与红山文化玉猪龙相似且具祭祀意义，是辽西地区最早的猪首龙原始形态[1]。阜新查海遗址发现的龙形堆石，位于聚落的中部，通长 19.7 米，其南侧分布墓葬和祭祀坑，推测为重要崇拜祭祀性神祇[2]。

---

[1] 中国社会科学院考古研究所内蒙古第一工作队：《内蒙古赤峰市兴隆沟聚落遗址 2002—2003 年的发掘》，《考古》2004 年第 7 期。
[2] 辽宁省文物考古研究所编著：《查海：新石器时代聚落遗址发掘报告》，文物出版社，2012 年。

兴隆洼文化遗址发现的与龙有关且具祭祀性质的遗迹表明，辽西地区远古先民在距今 8000 年前后对龙的崇拜已具图腾崇拜含义，崇拜形象由某些动物实体向抽象化转变。兴隆洼文化时期是龙文化的孕育期。

二、距今 5000 年前后龙形象的发展

中国农业起源可追溯至万年前，经历漫长的发展，至距今 7000 年前后，南稻北粟的农业格局业已形成。农作物播种的时间是否准确决定了收成的丰歉，观象授时在农耕文化中尤为重要，作为星象的龙与农时产生了密切联系。

（一）赵宝沟文化

兴隆洼文化结束之后，赵宝沟文化在辽西地区兴起。从房屋形制、聚落布局及出土遗物的特征看，赵宝沟文化是在直接承继兴隆洼文化的基础上发展起来的，其年代约为距今 7000—6400 年。尊形器是赵宝沟文化的典型陶器之一，在极少数尊形器的腹部刻划有复杂的动物纹饰。小山遗址出土的尊形器腹部刻划鸟兽纹饰，主体是鹿、猪、鸟的侧视形象。其中猪的形象用写实手法表现头部的长吻和獠牙，身体则为抽象的"S"形卷曲状，在头部和身体的接合处还刻划出向后飘逸的鬃鬣，形象逼真，应为辽西地区猪首龙形象成熟的标志[3]。以小山尊形器为代表，赵宝沟文化先民承继了兴隆洼文化先民对于动物崇拜的传统，并将其抽象化、图案化，崇拜野猪的习俗得到升华。将猪首龙的形象刻划在祭祀用的陶器上，是辽西地区龙文化形成的重要标志，为红山文化时期玉猪龙的出现奠定了重要基础。

（二）红山文化

红山文化因内蒙古赤峰市红山后遗址的发掘而得名。距今 5500—5000 年前后的红山文化晚期，人口迅猛增长，生产力水平显著提高，社会复杂化进程加快，出现了以牛河梁为代表的大型埋葬中心和祭祀中心，辽西地区进入初级文明社会。

龙形玉器是红山文化动物造型玉器中最具代表性的器类之一。红山文化龙形玉器根据造型特征可以分为两类：一类是"C"形玉龙，其造型具有典型的地域和时代风格，昂首，弯背，卷尾，整体造型呈"C"形，穿孔位于龙体中部；另一类是玉猪龙，体卷曲如环形，尾端漫收，头、尾明显分开、相距甚近或连接，头部较大，双耳竖立，眼、嘴、鼻线条清晰，双目圆睁，吻部前凸，有明显褶皱，嘴张开或闭拢。从造型特征和使用功能看，红山文化玉猪龙同兴隆洼文化早期"龙"文化因素和赵宝沟文化刻划而

---

[3] 中国社会科学院考古研究所内蒙古工作队：《内蒙古敖汉旗小山遗址》，《考古》1987 年第 6 期。

成的猪首龙形象一脉相承，对商周及后期玉龙的雕琢和崇龙礼俗的发展产生了重要影响。以红山文化玉龙的出现为标志，辽西地区龙文化的发展走向成熟。

龙是宗教祭祀发达的产物。红山文化积石冢代表一种特殊形式的埋葬制度，同时也是生者举行祭祀活动的场所，祭祀典礼的内容以祭天地、神灵、祖灵为主。张光直认为，中国上古宇宙观是把世界分为天、地、神、人等不同层次，并以巫者沟通天、地、神的活动作为宗教祭祀的主要内容，各类动物就是沟通天地的助手[4]。红山文化各种动物题材的玉器，应是巫者通神的工具。从这个角度分析，红山文化玉龙的出现，应是红山文化晚期宗教祭祀活动发展到一定阶段的产物。

辽西地区龙的孕育、形成和发展与远古先民的生产和生活密不可分。红山文化分布地区多为山地、丘陵，干旱是困扰农业生产的主要因素，祈雨活动应该是红山文化先民宗教祭祀活动中的重要内容之一，而红山文化玉龙的出现应与辽西地区旱作农业的发展及相应的祈雨活动紧密相关。

（三）凌家滩文化

凌家滩文化距今约 5800—5300 年，因安徽含山凌家滩遗址的发掘而得名。1998年，考古工作者于凌家滩遗址 M16 中挖掘出一件玉龙。该玉龙身体呈环形，首尾相互连接，头顶部有明显的双角，背部高高隆起形成脊状，脊上刻有均匀分布的短斜线纹，并且靠近尾端处有一个小孔。其造型独特，与红山文化的玉猪龙存在明显差异[5]。2022 年，考古人员又在凌家滩遗址有了新的发现，一件玉龙首形器得以重见天日。这件器物的头部形似猪首，在这一点上与红山文化玉猪龙有相近之处，然而其尾端呈尖锐状。这种造型的玉器在凌家滩文化中还是首次出现[6]，它为深入探究中国龙文化的起源及早期发展历程，提供了全新且极具价值的考古实证依据。

（四）良渚文化

良渚文化距今约 5300—4300 年，因浙江余杭良渚遗址的发现而得名，是长江下游地区环太湖流域最重要的新石器时代考古学文化之一。良渚文化玉器上多见有神人兽面纹，与之共出的还有一类纹样——龙首纹，在反山、瑶山玉器中有不少数量。这类图像无论正视还是侧视，都明确地显示了中国古代"龙"的特征。此外还发现有单体的玉龙，良渚遗址群官井头、余杭后头山、海宁皇坟头、海盐仙坛庙、昆山赵陵山

---

4 张光直：《考古学专题六讲（增订本）》，生活·读书·新知三联书店，2013 年。

5 安徽省文物考古研究所、含山县文物管理所：《安徽含山县凌家滩遗址第三次发掘简报》，《考古》1999 年第 11 期。

6 安徽省文物考古研究所、含山县凌家滩遗址管理处：《安徽含山凌家滩遗址考古取得重大收获》，《中国文物报》2022 年 12 月 8 日，第 5 版。

等遗址均有出土，数量不多，分布地域甚广，但主要集中在良渚遗址群及邻近区域，年代在崧泽文化晚期到良渚文化早期[7]。值得注意的是，玉龙的形态与远在上千公里之外的红山文化玉雕龙较为接近，可能表明这一时期存在着远程区域之间的"上层交流网"。

结合反山、瑶山等良渚遗址群内出土的大量龙首纹和龙首图案玉器，能够明确良渚遗址群是玉龙的重要出土地点。在这里，图像实现了从具象玉龙到图案化龙首纹的演变。进入良渚文化中晚期，玉龙的基本构成融入兽面纹之中，反映了该地区的原始宗教和信仰。

（五）陶寺文化

陶寺文化距今 4300—3900 年，因山西襄汾陶寺遗址的发掘而得名，遗址面积约 300 万平方米，是龙山文化晚期的一处大型中心聚落，也是中国史前时期"都城要素最完备"的城址[8]。彩绘龙纹陶盘是陶寺文化龙文物的代表。在已发掘的墓葬中，有 4 座大墓中各出土 1 件彩绘龙纹陶盘，该类陶盘应该为祭祀用器[9]。彩绘龙纹陶盘出土于大墓，结合陶寺遗址"最初中国"的考古背景，其图案被认为是早期象征王权的龙形象，这表明龙在当时可能与社会的统治阶层和权力结构相关联，体现了人们对王权的敬畏和崇拜。此外，龙口中衔着似禾苗的枝状物，鉴于陶寺文化处于比较发达的史前农业经济阶段，当时人种植的主要农作物包括粟、黍、稻和大豆等，这也体现了陶寺先民对农业生产的重视和对丰收的渴望。他们相信龙具有掌控自然气候、影响农作物生长的超自然力量，将龙作为祈求风调雨顺、农业丰收的象征。《周易·乾卦·文言》云："见龙在田，天下文明。"[10] 陶寺彩绘龙纹口衔禾苗的形象，反映了龙文化与农业文明之间的深刻联系，是文明肇始的生动诠释。

三、夏、商、西周时期龙形象的演变

夏、商、西周时期，中国早期文明从"多元"走向"一体"，特征统一的龙形象大量出现在高规格、高等级的墓葬中和器物上。

（一）夏时期

夏时期的龙形象主要雕刻于陶器上，或用绿松石镶嵌于青铜器和漆木器上，其中

---

7 方向明：《良渚玉器神人兽面像的真相》，《大众考古》2015 年第 6 期。

8 中国社会科学院考古研究所、山西省临汾市文物局编著：《襄汾陶寺——1978－1985 年考古发掘报告》，文物出版社，2015 年。

9 何驽：《蟠龙根脉——中华精神"图腾"的面世》，《十件文物里的中国故事》，中国社会科学出版社，2022 年。

10 （魏）王弼、（晋）韩康伯注，（唐）孔颖达疏：《周易正义》，上海古籍出版社，1990 年。

二里头遗址出土的嵌绿松石龙形器和龙纹铜牌饰是重要代表[11]。夏时期的龙形象在继承前代基础上发展，更加抽象、图案化，造型逐渐定型、完善，已具典型成熟龙形象特征。

河南新密新砦遗址是探索早期夏文化的重要遗址[12]。其出土的陶器盖残片上阴刻有龙纹，方头和"臣"字目的形态与二里头遗址出土绿松石龙有相似之处，应为其最直接的渊源或祖型。

河南偃师二里头遗址距今约3800—3500年，被普遍认为是夏王朝都城[13]。二里头遗址的嵌绿松石龙形器出土于2002ⅤM3，该墓是二里头文化早期目前已知规格最高的贵族墓葬。这件龙形器被放置于墓主的身上，呈拥揽状态。在田野考古发现之后，采用套箱整体起取，历经两年的实验室清理，揭露出龙形器的完整面貌。全器由2000余片绿松石组合而成，原应粘嵌在某种有机物上。龙身长64.5厘米，中部最宽处4厘米，巨头蜷尾。龙头置于绿松石片粘嵌而成的近梯形托座上，为扁圆形巨首，吻部略凸出。以三节青、白玉柱组成额面中脊和鼻梁。眼睛为梭形。眼眶内嵌绿松石片，以顶面弧凸的圆饼形白玉为睛。龙身近尾部渐变为圆弧隆起，尾尖内蜷。绿松石片象征鳞纹，遍布全身。龙尾端3.6厘米处，发现一件绿松石条形饰，与龙体近于垂直，二者之间有红色漆痕相连。在龙身中部有一件铜铃，铜铃内有玉质铃舌。《诗经》中记载宗庙祭祀时，有"龙旂阳阳，和铃央央"[14]的场景描写，其中"龙旂"与"和铃"并举，同该墓龙形器、铜铃共存的情况相吻合，因此龙形器有可能是夏代旌旗上装饰的升龙形象。墓主人应是供职于王朝的巫师，其所佩龙旌具有引领亡灵升天的宗教意义[15]。总之，二里头嵌绿松石龙形器用工之巨、制作之精、体量之大，在中国龙文化发展史上十分罕见，是夏时期最具代表性的龙形象文物。

（二）商时期

商时期是我国青铜时代的鼎盛时期，青铜器上的纹饰丰富多彩，龙纹是其中极为重要的组成部分。商时期龙纹在造型上呈现出多样化的特点，有夔龙纹、蟠龙纹等多种形式[16]。夔龙纹为侧面形象，一足或无足，以卷曲的线条和凌厉的角、目为特征，给人以威严神秘之感。蟠龙纹则呈卷曲盘旋状，身体上常饰有云雷纹等装饰元素，仿佛在青铜器表面游动。商时期青铜器上龙纹的大量出现，一方面反映了当时高超的青铜铸造技术，

[11] 朱乃诚：《二里头文化"龙"遗存研究》，《中原文物》2006年第4期。

[12] 北京大学震旦古代文明研究中心、郑州市文物考古研究院：《新密新砦——1999－2000年田野考古发掘报告》，文物出版社，2008年。

[13] 中国社会科学院考古研究所编著：《二里头（1999－2006）》，文物出版社，2014年。

[14] （汉）郑玄笺，（唐）孔颖达疏：《毛诗注疏》，上海古籍出版社，2013年。

[15] 许宏：《碧龙耀世——"超级国宝"的前世今生》，《十件文物里的中国故事》，中国社会科学出版社，2022年。

[16] 朱凤瀚：《中国青铜器综论》，上海古籍出版社，2009年。

另一方面也表明龙在商时期社会中的地位更加重要。龙纹在青铜器上的广泛应用，应与商时期的宗教祭祀和政治统治密切相关。商王可能认为自己与龙有着特殊的联系，通过在祭祀等礼仪场合使用的青铜器上装饰龙纹，来彰显其统治的合法性和权威性。

玉龙是商时期龙形象的另一项重要内容。商时期玉龙的形制多样，有圆雕玉龙、片状两面雕玉龙、璜形玉龙、玦形玉龙、珠状玉龙等[17]。妇好墓出土的半圆雕玉龙[18]，形制为首尾相对的勾卷状，吻部呈扁状前凸，头部呈扁平状，有双立耳，整体造型与新石器时代的玦形玉龙存在相似之处，体现龙形象与龙文化的传承和延续。

（三）西周时期

西周时期，龙纹在继承商时期风格的基础上又有了新的变化。龙纹是西周玉器上的重要装饰题材，西周时期龙纹玉器多为片状，作为佩饰的组成部分，在仪式场合穿戴佩挂。其中精美者如人龙合体纹饰佩[19]，利用圆弧曲线和琢磨成坡面的斜刀技巧，形成华丽流畅的视觉效果。人与龙相融合的主题，其用意在于表达人龙合一的神性[20]。

西周时期的龙纹整体上更加规整、细腻，线条更加流畅，造型上也更趋于图案化。与商时期龙纹相比，西周时期龙纹的神秘色彩略有减弱，而更多地体现出一种秩序感和规范性。这一变化可能与西周时期用玉观念的转变有关，商时期玉器主要用以表达宗教神权，而西周时期玉器则转变为阶级身份的象征。西周时期的龙纹反映了人们对社会秩序和礼仪规范的重视，龙形象的应用成为这种秩序和规范在艺术领域的象征之一。

四、春秋战国至秦汉时期龙形象的新发展

（一）春秋战国时期

春秋战国时期，龙的造型逐渐稳定，身躯多蜿蜒曲折，四足和尾部渐渐明晰，灵动矫健。龙与其他动物和植物纹样相融合，形成舞凤飞龙纹、龙凤虎纹等绚丽多彩的图案，具有浪漫主义美学风格，龙的神圣属性也得到彰显。

春秋战国时期的玉器制作工艺达到了一个新的高峰，龙形玉佩在这一时期大量涌现。这些龙形玉佩造型各异，有的呈回首状，有的呈腾飞状，线条流畅优美，工艺精湛绝伦。龙的身体上常常雕刻有谷纹、涡纹等来表现鳞片，使龙的形象更加华丽。龙形玉佩在这一时期不仅是一种装饰品，其在造型和风格上的多样化也反映了这一时期

---

[17] 朱乃诚：《商代玉龙研究》，《文博学刊》2021 年第 3 期。
[18] 中国社会科学院考古研究所编辑：《殷墟妇好墓》，文物出版社，1980 年。
[19] 中国社会科学院考古研究所编著：《张家坡西周玉器》，文物出版社，2007 年。
[20] 蔡庆良：《商、西周玉器风格比较》，《紫禁城》2010 年第 3、4 期。

地域文化的繁荣和多元。湖北荆州院墙湾一号楚墓出土有一件人执龙形玉佩[21]，两侧为相向而立的双龙，龙背上各站立一鸟，为楚地流行的龙的形象；中间的一人着紧袖长袍，袍上饰二方连续间隔长方形网纹，为中山国北狄服饰。因此这件玉佩有可能是由楚国玉工制作，但受到中山国玉文化的影响。

此时的龙还受到了北方草原地带人群的喜爱。内蒙古杭锦旗阿鲁柴登墓葬出土有一件金冠饰，是游牧部落首领的饰物。冠饰由冠顶和冠带组成，冠顶浮雕有四狼吃羊的图案，中央为立鹰；冠带装饰有卧羊、卧马和龙，龙首似狼似虎，具有鲜明的草原文化风格。

（二）秦汉时期

在秦汉大一统王朝时期，龙的象征意义更加丰富和明确。自秦汉开始，龙被视为皇权的象征，秦始皇嬴政自称为"祖龙"[22]，汉高祖刘邦被称为"赤帝子"[23]。这一时期龙的形象在继承前代的基础上，更加生动多变，增加了髯和肘鬣，发展出了龙翼，更显威武。徐州狮子山汉墓出土有多件龙形玉佩，基本延续了战国时期的风格，龙身虬曲，龙首雕刻精致[24]。汉代的画像石、画像砖以及漆器、丝绸等都大量运用了龙的形象，往往与云气、仙人等元素结合在一起，乘龙升天等题材普遍流行，体现了汉代人对神仙世界的向往和追求。

同时，渊源于史前时期的"四神"概念在汉代也已定型，"苍龙连蜷于左，白虎猛踞于右，朱雀奋翼于前，灵龟圈首于后"[25]成为定制。汉长安城发现有多件四神瓦当[26]，其中青龙瓦当的龙形态呈奔走状，矫健有力。云南罗平汉墓出土的博局纹铜镜也饰有"四神"，并搭配羽人、凤鸟等纹饰，反映了中原文化对西南地区的影响。

秦汉时期的龙形象昂扬奔放，生动自由，气势磅礴，在中国龙文化发展史上占有极其重要的地位。

五、魏晋至隋唐时期龙形象的多元融汇

魏晋南北朝时期，龙的形象在整体上与汉代有着诸多相似之处，亦呈现出魏晋风度。北方的龙矫健敦实、蕴含张力，南方的龙丰盈修长、飘逸如仙。龙翼多呈飘动的火焰状，或称之为"肘鬣膊焰"，常常表现出一种腾飞而起的姿态。

---

[21] 荆州博物馆：《湖北荆州院墙湾一号楚墓》，《文物》2008 年第 4 期。

[22]（汉）司马迁撰：《史记》卷六《秦始皇本纪》，中华书局，1959 年。

[23]（汉）司马迁撰：《史记》卷八《高祖本纪》，中华书局，1959 年。

[24] 狮子山楚王陵考古发掘队：《徐州狮子山西汉楚王陵发掘简报》，《文物》1998 年第 8 期。韦正、李虎仁、邹厚本：《江苏徐州市狮子山西汉墓的发掘与收获》，《考古》1998 年第 8 期。

[25]（南朝宋）范晔撰：《后汉书》志第十《天文上》，中华书局，1965 年。

[26] 中国社会科学院考古研究所编著：《西汉礼制建筑遗址》，文物出版社，2003 年。

尽管这一时期战乱频繁，社会生活遭到了严重破坏，但多元的思想文化尤其是佛教的影响为龙的形象加入了新的因素。内蒙古包头市达茂旗西河子出土一件金龙形项饰[27]，龙身用金丝编缀成绞索式，缀有两盾、两戟和一钺，两端各有一金片卷制的龙头，龙角以金丝缠绕。这件形似璎珞的项饰即为"五兵佩"，在魏晋时期流行，《晋书·五行志》说："惠帝元康中，妇人之饰有五兵佩，又以金银玳瑁之属，为斧钺戈戟，以当笄。"[28]这件项饰混合了斯基泰、犍陀罗等诸种工艺手法，反映了当时多元文化相互交融的历史风貌。

隋唐时期，国家统一，社会安定，龙的姿态也愈发奔放雄健，气韵生动。这一时期以行龙最为常见，或走或坐或飞，动静之中蕴含着力量和刚健，充分体现出盛世气象。丝绸之路的繁荣促进了中外文化的交流，联珠纹等外来文化元素与龙的主题相结合，达到了新的艺术高度。

河南偃师杏园唐墓中出土的三彩龙柄壶盛行于初唐和盛唐时期，多见于西安和洛阳地区[29]。龙形柄细长，龙嘴衔于壶口，线条优美流畅，一方面承袭了西晋以后鸡首壶的传统，另一方面则反映出罗马和波斯文化的影响，体现了多种文化因素的交融和互鉴[30]。金质龙纹马鞍饰出土于青海都兰热水墓群2018血渭一号墓。器身上捶揲有多种动植物纹样，其中右侧的主体纹样为一立龙，龙身修长，龙首昂起，口吐云气。2018血渭一号墓的墓主可能是吐谷浑王莫贺吐浑可汗[31]，这件精美的马鞍饰既是吐谷浑王陵的等级标志，也是丝绸之路青海道的历史见证。

六、宋元明清时期龙形象的广泛传播

宋代是我国古代文化艺术的一个发展高峰，龙的形态在此时基本定型。南宋《尔雅翼》记载，龙"有三停九似之说，谓自首至膊，膊至腰，腰至尾，皆相停也。九似者，角似鹿，头似驼，眼似兔，颈似蛇，腹似蜃，鳞似鱼，爪似鹰，掌似虎，耳似牛"[32]，即为后世常见的龙的形象。宋代的龙纹洗练洒脱，刻画细腻，常穿插于祥云、海浪、花草之间，上下翻腾，富于变化，与当时的审美意趣相契合。南宋陈容的《九龙图》将九条姿态各异的龙绘于险山云雾、巨浪潮水中，遨游追逐，或隐或现。其精湛多变

27 陆思贤、陈棠栋：《达茂旗出土古代北方民族金龙等贵重文物》，《内蒙古社会科学》1983年第4期。
28 （唐）房玄龄等撰：《晋书》，中华书局，1974年。
29 中国社会科学院考古研究所编著：《偃师杏园唐墓》，科学出版社，2001年。
30 赵德云：《从鸡头壶到龙柄壶的发展——兼析外来文化因素在这一过程中的作用》，《考古与文物》2007年第1期。
31 中国社会科学院考古研究所、青海省文物考古研究所：《青海都兰县热水墓群2018血渭一号墓》，《考古》2021年第8期。
32 （宋）罗愿撰，石云孙校点：《尔雅翼》，黄山书社，2013年。

的笔法、错落有致的构图、生动传神的情态刻画将这一时期龙的特点表现得淋漓尽致，成为后世的典范。河南洛阳宋园遗址出土有一件陶龙形脊饰[33]，细长纤秀，形象华丽，是高等级建筑的象征。辽、金、西夏则基本沿用唐代龙的形象。内蒙古赤峰阿鲁科尔沁旗的耶律羽之墓出土有一件鎏金盘龙镜[34]，龙身雄健有力，既是墓主贵族身份的象征，亦是辽承唐风的体现。

元代的龙纹与宋代较为相似，身形较细长，原来长着象征性羽翼的位置，已被宛曲多叉的火焰纹替代，有的龙尾添上尾鳍，风格简洁古朴。元代的龙纹应用广泛，尤其在瓷器上得到了淋漓尽致的表现。以青花瓷器为代表，其上绘制的龙纹色彩鲜艳丰富，层次分明，生动传神。内蒙古赤峰市林西县发现的青花龙纹高足杯和青花龙纹盘，细颈三爪，身形流畅，鳞片细腻，与周围的草叶纹、缠枝纹、云纹相得益彰，使画面更为丰富。北京元大都遗址出土有一件白地黑花龙凤纹瓷扁壶[35]，白地黑花是宋元时期北方地区流行的瓷器品种，扁壶的造型又兼具草原民族特征。此时龙的等级含义也被进一步加强，元代的统治者对龙的使用进行了限制，双角五爪的龙成为皇权的象征。

至明清时期，龙形象广泛应用于建筑、陶瓷、刺绣等社会生活的各个领域。明代编撰了"龙生九子"的故事[36]，为早已存在的各类龙形神兽正名并赋予其龙种的身份，丰富了龙文化的内涵。至明代中晚期，出现了正面脸的正龙纹，成为皇家御用的图案。它不仅是一种装饰，更是一种文化符号和政治象征，代表着皇权的至高无上，反映了社会的等级制度和统治秩序。清代继续沿用这种徽章式的正龙纹，繁缛华贵、精巧富丽的五爪金龙被装饰在龙袍、龙椅、龙床上，作为皇权的象征，代表着权力和威严。在民间，龙文化也深入人心，各种与龙有关的民俗丰富多彩，舞龙灯、赛龙舟等活动在民间广泛开展，成为人们庆祝节日、祈求吉祥的重要方式，流传至今。

七、龙形象的内涵与意义

（一）宗教与信仰意义

从8000年前龙形象的起源来看，龙最初可能与原始宗教信仰有关。新石器时代中期的远古先民将龙视为一种具有超自然力量的存在，认为其能够掌控风雨、山川等自然元素。在祭祀活动中，龙形象可能是沟通人与神灵的媒介，人们通过对龙的崇拜和祭祀来祈求神灵的庇佑和恩赐。随着时间的推移，龙在不同文化时期的宗教信仰体系中

---

[33] 中国社会科学院考古研究所编著：《隋唐洛阳城：1959—2001年考古发掘报告》，文物出版社，2014年。
[34] 内蒙古文物考古研究所、赤峰市博物馆、阿鲁科尔沁旗文物管理所：《辽耶律羽之墓发掘简报》，《文物》1996年第1期。
[35] 中国社会科学院考古研究所、北京市文物管理处编著：《元大都——1964—1974年考古报告》，文物出版社，2024年。
[36]（明）李东阳撰：《怀麓堂集》，上海古籍出版社，1991年。

扮演着不同的角色，但始终是与神灵、祖先崇拜等相关联的重要元素。

（二）政治与权力象征

龙与政治权力的联系在历史发展过程中逐渐加强。从红山文化玉龙可能象征着社会上层权力开始，到商周时期龙纹在青铜器上体现王权统治，再到秦汉时期龙成为皇权的象征，龙在政治领域的象征意义越来越明确。统治者将龙与自己的身份相联系，通过龙的形象来强化自己的统治权威，使民众对其统治产生敬畏之心。龙作为政治权力象征的这一内涵，在封建王朝时期一直延续并不断强化。

（三）文化与民族精神象征

龙文化贯穿于中华民族的历史长河，成为中华民族文化和民族精神的重要象征。龙所代表的吉祥、权威、力量等含义，反映了中华民族对美好生活的向往和追求，以及对自身民族的自豪感和认同感。龙文化融合了中华民族各个历史时期的思想、信仰和价值观，在文学、艺术、民俗等各个领域均产生了广泛的影响，是中华民族凝聚力和向心力的重要体现。

通过对新石器时代至明清时期考古发现的龙形象文物的梳理，可以清晰地看到中国龙文化的发展脉络，从简单的原始崇拜象征逐渐发展成为政治权力、宗教信仰和民族精神的重要符号，其内涵丰富而深刻。8000 年来，龙文化以其独特的魅力在中华大地上传承和发展，对中华民族的形成、发展和文化传承产生了不可估量的作用。龙作为中华民族的图腾，充分体现了中华文明突出的连续性、创新性、统一性、包容性、和平性。它不仅是中华民族历史文化的瑰宝，更是中华民族在世界文化之林中独特身份的重要标志。

中国考古博物馆

2025 年 1 月 5 日

Introduction

China's 8000 Years Loong Culture
from an Archaeological Perspective

As a unique cultural symbol of the Chinese nation, the loong culture has a far-reaching and wide-ranging influence. President Xi Jinping pointed out in his important speech at the Spring Festival reception in the Year of the Loong that as the totem of the Chinese nation, the loong is deemed strong, fearless, benevolent, and powerful. The origins of Chinese loong culture trace back to ancient times. As early as the Neolithic period, many archaeological discoveries related to loongs have been made across China. With the progress of archaeological research, an increasing number of artifacts have provided solid evidence of the development and continuity of loong culture in Chinese history. Exploring the origins and evolution of loong culture helps us gain a deeper understanding of the Chinese people's early spiritual beliefs, social organization, and cultural exchanges.

The Origin of Loong Image Around 8,000 Years Ago

Entering the Neolithic Age, our ancestors had already characterized loongs based on their familiar animal images, reflecting unique aesthetics and beliefs. Xinglongwa culture sites are the most representative. The Xinglongwa culture is an important archaeological culture of the Neolithic Age in western Liaoning, with its origins dating from approximately 8,200 years ago. The Xinglongwa culture established the central role of the West Liaohe River Basin in the development of Neolithic culture in the Northeast region. Its sites include Aohan Banner Xinglongwa, Xinglonggou, Hexigten Banner Nantaizi, Linxi Baiyinchanghan, Fuxin Chahai and so on. The Xinglonggou site location No.1 is a large-scale settlement in the middle of Xinglongwa culture, in which the *S*-shape remains with a boar's head found in the H35 sacrificial pit is similar to the jade coiled loong of Hongshan culture and has ritual significance, which is the earliest primitive form of the loong with a boar's head in western Liaoning area. The loong-shaped pile of stones found in the Fuxin Chahai site is located in the middle of the settlement, with a total length of 19.7 meters. The burials and sacrificial pits on the south side of the pile are presumed to be important for the worship of sacrificial gods and goddesses.

Archaeological remains with sacrificial significance related to loongs discovered at the Xinglongwa culture site indicate that around 8,000 years ago, ancient communities in western Liaoning revered loongs as totemic symbols. Over time, this veneration transitioned from realistic depictions of animals to more abstract forms. The Xinglongwa culture period can be seen as the early stage in the development of the loong culture.

The Development of Loong Image Around 5,000 Years Ago

The origin of agriculture in China can be traced back 10,000 years. The agricultural pattern of rice in the south and millet in the north underwent a long development and was formed around 7,000 years ago. The exact timing of sowing crops determines the amount of harvest. Determining the time by observing the celestial movements of the sun, moon, and stars was particularly important in farming culture. As an astrological sign, the loong is closely related to the farming timetable.

Zhaobaogou Culture

After the end of the Xinglongwa culture, the Zhaobaogou culture emerged in western Liaoning. Based on the characteristics of the housing structure, settlement layout, and excavated relics, the Zhaobaogou culture was developed based on directly inheriting the Xinglongwa culture, and it can be dated back 7,000 to 6,400 years before the present. The *zun*-shaped vessel is one of the typical pottery of the Zhaobaogou culture, and in very few cases, the belly of the vessel is engraved with complex animal patterns. This vessel unearthed at the Xiaoshan site is decorated with animal motifs on its belly, and the central part of the motifs is a side view of a deer, a boar, and a bird. The image of the boar is a realistic representation of the head with a long muzzle and tusk, an abstract *S*-shaped body, and a realistic mane. It is a sign of the maturity of the image of the boar-headed loong in western Liaoning. Represented by the Xiaoshan *zun*-shaped vessel, the ancestors of the Zhaobaogou culture inherited the tradition of animal worship from the ancestors in the Xinglongwa culture and abstracted and patterned it. The custom of worshipping wild boars was elevated. The image of a boar-headed loong engraved on ritual pottery is an important symbol of the formation of the loong culture in West Liaohe River Reaches, laying an important foundation for the emergence of the jade coiled loong in the Hongshan culture.

Hongshan Culture

The Hongshan culture was named after the Hongshanhou site in Chifeng, Inner Mongolia

Autonomous Region. About 5,500 to 5,000 years ago, in the late Hongshan culture, the population grew rapidly, productivity level increased significantly, social complexity accelerated, and large-scale burial centers and ritual centers represented by Niuheliang emerged. The western Liaoning area became a civilized society.

Loong-shaped jade artifacts are one of the most iconic types of animal-shaped jade from the Hongshan Culture. These jade loongs can be categorized into two primary styles based on their design features. The first is the *C*-shaped jade loong, which showcases a distinctive regional and temporal style. This loong is depicted with its head raised, back arched, and tail curled, forming an alphabet *C* shape, with a hole placed in the middle of the body. The second type is the jade coiled loong, which curls into a circular form with a tapered tail. Its head and tail are clearly separated, often positioned close together or even connected. The head is larger, with upright ears and distinct features such as clearly defined eyes, mouth, and nose lines. The snout is protruding with noticeable wrinkles, and the mouth may be either open or closed.

In terms of design and function, the jade coiled loong from the Hongshan culture continues the loong-related motifs seen in the early loong culture of the Xinglongwa culture and the boar-headed loong figures of the Zhaobaogou culture. This tradition had a lasting influence on the carving of jade loongs during the Shang and Zhou Dynasties, as well as the development of loong worship rituals. The appearance of the Hongshan culture jade loong marks the point at which loong culture in the western Liaoning reached maturity.

The loong is a result of well-developed religious rituals. The Hongshan culture stone mound tombs represent a special form of burial system, and they were also places for the living to hold ritual activities. The contents of the sacrificial ceremonies were mainly dedicated to heaven and earth, gods, and ancestral spirits. Chang Kwuang-chi argues that ancient Chinese cosmology divided the world into different levels, such as heaven, earth, gods, and human beings, and took the Shaman's activities of communicating with heaven, earth, and gods as the main content of religious sacrifices. Various kinds of animals were the assistants of communication between heaven and earth. The function of the jade objects with various animal themes in the Hongshan culture was to serve as tools for the Shaman to communicate with the gods. Analyzed from this perspective, the appearance of jade loongs in the Hongshan culture is a product of the development of religious ritual activities to a certain extent in the late Hongshan culture.

The emergence, formation, and development of loongs in western Liaoning are inseparable from the production activities and lives of the ancient ancestors. The area of Hongshan culture is primarily mountainous and hilly. Drought was the main factor plaguing agricultural production. Praying for rain was one of the important contents of the religious rituals held by the ancestors of the Hongshan culture, and the appearance of the jade loong of the Hongshan culture is closely related to the development of dry farming system and the corresponding praying for rain in western Liaoning.

Lingjiatan Culture

The Lingjiatan culture, which dates from about 5,800 to 5,300 years ago, is named after the Lingjiatan site in Hanshan, Anhui Province. In 1998, archaeologists excavated a jade loong in tomb No.16 of the Lingjiatan site. The loong has a ring-shaped body with an interconnected head and tail, two horns growing from the top of the head, and a raised back decorated with carved lines, and there is a small hole near the tail end. Its shape is unique and differs significantly from that of the coiled loong of the Hongshan culture. In 2022, archaeologists discovered a new jade object with a loong head at the Lingjiatan site. The head of this loong is like a boar's head, which is similar to that of the jade coiled loong in Hongshan culture, but with a sharp end. This is the first time archaeologists found a jade object of this shape in the Lingjiatan culture.

Liangzhu Culture

Liangzhu culture, dating from 5300 to 4300 years ago, is named after the discovery of the Liangzhu site in Yuhang, Zhejiang Province. It is one of the most important Neolithic archaeological cultures in the area around Taihu Lake in the lower reaches of the Yangtze River. The Liangzhu culture jade artifacts are mostly characterized by human-animal deity face motifs, with which there is another type of motif, loong head motifs, which account for many jade artifacts found at the Fanshan and Yaoshan sites. These images, whether viewed from the front or from the side, clearly show the characteristics of the ancient Chinese loong. In addition, there are also artifacts of jade loong excavated in Liangzhu site group such as Guanjingtou site, Yuhang Houtoushan site, Haining Huangfentou site, Haiyan Xiantanmiao site, Kunshan Zhaolingshan site, and other sites. The number of these jade loongs is not significant. Although it is scattered in a wide range of geographical areas, it is concentrated in the Liangzhu site group and the adjacent areas, dating from the late Songze culture to the early Liangzhu culture. Notably, the form of the jade loongs is almost identical to that of the carved jade loongs of the Hongshan culture, thousands of kilometers away, which may indicate the existence of a "network of communication" among high hierarchy in remote regions during this period.

Combined with the large number of jade objects with loong head motifs and loong head designs unearthed within the Liangzhu site group, such as Fanshan and Yaoshan, the Liangzhu site group was important excavation sites for jade loongs. The images evolved from figurative jade loongs to patterned loong head motifs. Entering the middle and late Liangzhu culture, the elemental composition of the jade loong was integrated into the animal face pattern. At this time, the animal-face motifs of Liangzhu jade artifacts can also be regarded as loongs, reflecting the primitive religions and beliefs of the region.

Taosi Culture

Taosi culture, which dates back 4300 to 3900 years, was named the Taosi site in Xiangfen, Shanxi Province. The site, which has an area of about 3 million square meters, is a large central settlement in the late Longshan culture. It also contains the "most complete elements of the capital city" of China's prehistoric period. The painted pottery plate with loong design is a representative of the loong artifacts of the Taosi culture. In the excavated tombs, four large tombs each yielded a painted pottery plate featuring loong motifs, likely used in rituals. These plates, discovered in the context of the Taosi site—known as the "cradle of early Chinese civilization"—are thought to symbolize early royal authority. This suggests that the loong was closely tied to the ruling elite and power structures of the time, embodying awe and reverence for authority. Furthermore, the loong is depicted holding branch-like objects resembling seedlings in its mouth. Given that the Taosi culture flourished during a period of advanced prehistoric agriculture, with millet, broomcorn millet, rice, and soybeans as staple crops, this imagery reflects the community's focus on farming and their hopes for bountiful harvests. The people believed that the loong wielded supernatural power over weather and crop growth, making it a symbol of prayers for good weather and agricultural prosperity. The depiction of a loong holding seedlings vividly represents the deep connection between loong culture and agricultural life, offering a striking glimpse into the dawn of civilization.

The Evolution of Loong Image During the Xia, Shang, and Western Zhou Periods

During the Xia, Shang, and Western Zhou periods, early Chinese civilization gradually shifted from cultural diversity to a unified identity. Loong motifs with standardized designs became widespread, appearing prominently in elite tombs and on high-status artifacts.

Xia Period

In the Xia period, loong motifs were often carved onto pottery or inlaid with turquoise on bronze and lacquered wooden artifacts. Notable examples include the turquoise-inlaid loong and the bronze plaques with loong designs discovered at the Erlitou site. These designs were built on earlier traditions and became more abstract and stylized. Over time, loong imagery in this period became increasingly standardized and refined, showcasing the distinctive and mature features of what would become the classical loong motif.

The Xinzhai site in Xinmi, Henan Province, is a crucial site for exploring early Xia culture. A fragment of a pottery lid found at the site is engraved with a loong design featuring a square-shaped head and eye patterns resembling the shape of the "𦣞" character. This design shows a strong resemblance to the turquoise-inlaid loong discovered at the Erlitou site, suggesting it may have been a direct precursor or prototype for the Erlitou loong motif.

The Erlitou site in Yanshi, Henan Province, dating back roughly 3,800 to 3,500 years, is widely believed to be the capital of the Xia period. Among its most remarkable discoveries is a turquoise-inlaid loong unearthed in tomb 2002VM3, the highest-ranking noble tomb from the early Erlitou culture. This loong-shaped piece was placed on the tomb occupant's body in an embracing posture. After being excavated intact, it underwent two years of careful cleaning in the lab to reveal its full form. The artifact is composed of over 2,000 turquoise pieces, originally inlaid onto an organic base. Measuring 64.5 cm in length and 4 cm at its widest point, the loong features a large head and a coiled tail. Its flat, oval-shaped head rests on a near-trapezoidal turquoise base, with the snout slightly protruding. Three jade segments form the central ridge and nasal bridge. The almond-shaped eyes are outlined with turquoise inlays, and convex white jade discs serve as the pupils. The body rises into an arc near the tail, which curls inward at the tip, while turquoise pieces arranged across its surface represent scales. Near the tail's tip, a turquoise strip was found, positioned almost perpendicular to the body and connected by traces of red lacquer. In the midsection, a bronze bell containing a jade clapper was also discovered. The *Shijing* (*Classic of Poetry*) describes scenes of ancestral worship with the loong banner stood tall with its vivid design, as the chariot bells chimed with a melodious ring, paralleling the combination of this loong design and the bronze bell in the tomb. This suggests the artifact may have been part of a ceremonial loong banner used during the Xia period. The tomb occupant is believed to have been a shaman serving the royal court, with the loong banner symbolizing a spiritual role in guiding souls to the heavens. This turquoise-inlaid loong, with its intricate design, exceptional craftsmanship, and large size, is a rare and iconic artifact of the Xia period. It stands as a significant milestone in the development of Chinese loong culture.

Shang Period

The Shang period is the apex of China's Bronze Age, known for its extraordinary variety of decorative motifs on bronze artifacts, among which loong motifs held a place of great importance. Loong designs from this period came in diverse forms, with notable examples including the *kui*-loong and coiled-loong patterns. The *kui*-loong design depicts a side-profile loong, often with one or no legs, characterized by flowing, curved lines, sharp horns, and striking eyes that convey an aura of power and mystery. On the other hand, the coiled loong pattern features a spiraling form, with its body often embellished with a cloud-and-thunder pattern, giving the impression of a loong in motion across the bronze surface. The extensive use of loong motifs on Shang bronzes reflects not only the advanced bronze casting techniques of the era but also the elevated status of loongs in Shang society. The prevalence of these designs is closely tied to the Shang period's religious rituals and political system. Shang kings may have considered themselves embodiments of loongs or claimed a special connection to them. By incorporating loong imagery into ritual and ceremonial bronzes, they underscored their legitimacy and reinforced their ruling authority.

Jade loongs were an important aspect of Shang period loong imagery, crafted in a variety of styles. These included sculpted jade loongs, flat double-sided carvings, *huang*-shaped jade loongs, *jue*-shaped jade loongs, and bead-like jade loongs. One remarkable example is the semi-sculpted jade loong discovered in the Fuhao tomb. Its design features a hooked shape with the head and tail curving toward each other, a flat, protruding snout, and wide, upright ears on a flattened head. This form closely resembles the *jue*-shaped jade loongs of the Neolithic period, highlighting the enduring legacy and cultural continuity of loong symbolism across eras.

Western Zhou Period

In the Western Zhou period, loong motifs evolved while retaining elements of the Shang period style. These designs became a central decorative theme on jade artifacts, which were often flat in shape and used as ornaments for ceremonial attire. One exquisite example is the human-loong hybrid pendant. Its design uses flowing curves and a bevel-carving technique to create a smooth and elegant visual effect. The fusion of human and loong imagery reflects a divine connection and a sense of supernatural power.

Loong motifs in the Western Zhou period became more refined and symmetrical, with smoother lines and a more stylized, patterned appearance. Unlike the Shang period, where loong patterns carried a strong sense of mystery, Western Zhou designs shifted toward reflecting order and structure. This change was likely influenced by the evolution in the conceptualization of jade usage during the Western Zhou period. While jade artifacts primarily served to express religious and divine authority in the Shang period, they subsequently transformed into symbols representing social hierarchy and status during the Western Zhou era. The loong designs have mirrored this emphasis on social order and ritual propriety, with loong imagery symbolizing these values in the realm of art and decoration.

New Development of Loong Image
from Spring and Autumn and Warring States Periods
to Qin and Han Dynasties

Spring and Autumn and Warring States Periods

During the Spring and Autumn and Warring States periods, the shape of the loong was gradually explicit, with a sinuous body, four legs, and a tail. The loong was fused with other animal and plant motifs to form colorful patterns, such as phoenix, loong, and tiger, which construct a romantic aesthetic style, highlighting the sacred attributes of the loong.

Jade craftsmanship in the Spring and Autumn and Warring States periods reached a new peak, and loong-shaped jade pendants proliferated during this period. These jade pendants depicted different postures of the loongs. Some are looking back or flying above the ground, with beautiful streamlines and exquisite craftsmanship. Their body is often carved with grain and swirl decorations to represent the scales, making the loong look more dedicated. The loong-shaped jade pendant was not only used as a decorative object, but its varying shape and style also reflected the prosperity and diversity of regional cultures during this period. A jade pendant with a human reining loong design was unearthed from Yuanqiangwan Tomb No. 1 in Jingzhou, Hubei Province. It depicts two loongs standing oppositely on two sides, with a bird on the back of the loong, which is a popular loong image in Chu; one man is standing in the middle wearing a tight-sleeved robe decorated with a rectangular grid pattern, which is a typical nomadic costume of the Zhongshan State. Therefore, this jade pendant probably was made by Chu jade workers but was influenced by the jade culture of the Zhongshan State.

At this time, the loong was also favored by the people of northern nomadic groups. A gold crown ornament with an eagle-shaped top was excavated from Aluchaideng Tomb in Hanggin Banner, Inner Mongolia Autonomous Region, belonging to a nomadic tribal chief. The crown decoration is composed of a crown and bands. On the top are four wolves eating sheep pattern, the center of the standing eagle. The crown band is decorated with reclining sheep, horses, and loongs, and the loong head absorbs characteristics of wolf and tiger, sharing a distinctive style of nomadic culture.

Qin and Han Dynasties

The symbolism of the loong was enriched and clarified during the Qin and Han Dynasties. Since then, the loong was regarded as a symbol of imperial power. In this period, the loong image was mightier and more varied on the basis of inheriting the previous characteristics, adding the beard, elbow mane, and wings. A number of loong-shaped jade pendants have been unearthed from the Shizishan Han Tomb in Xuzhou, basically continuing the style of the Warring States period, with a gnarled body and an exquisitely carved head. In the Han Dynasty, the loong image was widely used in stone, brick, lacquerware, and silk, which were often combined with elements such as clouds and immortals. Themes such as riding the loong to heaven were popular, reflecting the pursuit of the celestial world.

At the same time, the concept of "four gods (mythical creatures)", which originated in prehistoric times, also took shape in the Han Dynasty: the Azure Loong of the East, the White Tiger of the West, the Vermilion Bird of the South, and the Black Tortoise of the North. Many four gods pattern tile-ends have been found in the Chang'an City of the Han Dynasty, among which is the Azure Loong tile-end, which has a running loong full of power. One bronze mirror excavated from the Han Tomb in Luoping, Yunan Province, also has four mythical creatures, feathered figures, phoenixes, and birds design, reflecting the influence of the Central Plains culture on the Southwest China region.

The loong image in the Qin and Han Dynasties was spirited and majestic, and it had a profound impact on the formation of the spiritual symbols of the Chinese nation in later generations.

The Multiple Integration of Loong Image from the Wei and Jin Dynasties to the Sui and Tang Dynasties

During the Wei, Jin, and Northern and Southern Dynasties, the loong image shared many similarities with the Han Dynasty at the same time and also showed the style of Wei and Jin Dynasties. The loongs in the north were robust and vigorous; the loongs in the south were slender and flowing. The loong's wings are primarily in the shape of flames, and their elbows have tidy manes, showing a gesture of rising over the ground.

Despite the frequent wars and destructions of society during this period, the influence of diverse ideas and cultures, especially Buddhism, added new elements to the image of the loong. A loong-shaped gold necklace was excavated from Xihezi, Darhan Muminggan United Banner, Baotou City, Inner Mongolia Autonomous Region. The loong's body is braided with gold wire as a chain, decorated with two shields, halberds, and a battle-axe miniature. At each end is a loong's head made of rolled gold thin sheets, with the horns entwined with gold wire. The design of the necklace, called "*Wubingpei*", prevailed in China during the Wei and Jin periods. This necklace employed Scythian, Gandharan, and other craft techniques, reflecting a vibrant multicultural history.

During the Sui and Tang Dynasties, with the unification of the country and the stabilization of society, the loong's posture became increasingly untrammeled and vigorous. Walking loong is the most common posture in this period. They often walk or fly, demonstrating strength and robustness in static and dynamic forms, fully embodying society's prosperity. The prosperity of the Silk Road promoted cultural exchanges between China and foreign countries, and the combination of foreign cultural elements, such as the Linked-pearl motif and the loong theme, reached new artistic heights.

The tri-coloured ewer with loong-shaped handle excavated from Xingyuan tombs in Yanshi, Henan Province, was prevalent in the early and middle Tang periods and is mostly found in the Xi'an and Luoyang regions. The loong-shaped handle is slender, and the loong's mouth is attached to the rim of the ewer's mouth. This design, on the one hand, inherits the tradition of pitchers since the Western Jin Dynasty, and on the other hand, reflects the influence of the Roman and Persian cultures, showing mutual learning among different cultures. A gold saddle decoration with loong design was unearthed from the 2018 Excavation of Xuewei Tomb No.1, Reshui Tomb Cluster, Dulan, Qinghai Province. The saddle is decorated with various animal and plant motifs, the main motif on the right side being a standing loong raising its head with a slender body. The tomb occupant could have been the Mohe Tuhun Khan. This exquisite saddle is a sign to prove the mausoleum belonging to the king of Tuyuhun and as a witness of the Silk Road Qinghai Road.

Widespread Loong Image in the Song, Yuan, Ming and Qing Dynasties

The Song Dynasty was a peak in the development of China's ancient culture and art, and the form of the loong was identified at this time. Southern Song Dynasty laid down the basic image of a loong, which is more common today. Based on the Southern Song Dynasty dictionary *Eryayi*, "the three parts of the loong are equal in length from head to forelimbs, from forelimbs to waist, and from waist to tail. In addition, a loong contains nine resemblances, they are following: antlers resemble those of a stag, head that of a camel, eyes those of a rabbit, neck that of a snake, belly that of a clam, scales those of a carp, claws those of an eagle, soles those of a tiger, ears those of a cattle". The loongs of the Song Dynasty were unrestrained and delicate, often interspersed with auspicious clouds, waves, flowers, and plants, tumbling up and down, full of changes. Southern Song painter Chen Rong's painting, *Nine Loongs*, depicts nine loongs with different postures in the mountains, clouds, and fog. They are swimming or chasing, hiding their body in waves or tides. It vividly portrays the loong's characteristics during this period, which has become the paradigm for the future. A slender and gorgeous pottery roof decoration in the shape of loong excavated from the site of Songyuan in Luoyang of Henan province symbolized high-level architecture. Liao, Jin, and Western Xia are basically along the image of the Tang Dynasty loong. The loong pattern from a gilded-gold bronze mirror with loong design excavated from the Tomb of Yelvyuzhi in Chifeng of Inner Mongolia Autonomous Region is strong and powerful, showing the aristocratic status of the tomb owner and reflecting the artistic style inherited from the Tang Dynasty.

The loong motifs of the Yuan Dynasty are similar to those of the Song Dynasty, in a simple and primitive style. The loong usually has an elongated body, flame motifs have replaced the original position with symbolic wings, and some loongs have caudal fins on their tails. The loong pattern of the Yuan Dynasty was widely used, especially in porcelain. The loong pattern is colorful and vivid, represented by blue and white porcelain. The loong pattern from both blue and white porcelain stem cup and plate with loong design found in Linxi County, Chifeng City, Inner Mongolia Autonomous Region, have thin necks, three claws, and delicate scales, surrounded by patterns of grass and leaves, entwined branches, and clouds. A white glazed porcelain flat flask with loong and phoenix design has been excavated from the site of Yuandadu in Beijing. Such type of porcelain was a popular porcelain variety in the northern region during the Song and Yuan

Dynasties, and the shape of the flat flask also reflects the characteristic of nomadic culture. The hierarchical meaning of the loong was further strengthened at this time. The rulers of the Yuan Dynasty restricted the use of loongs, and the two-horned, five-clawed loong became a symbol of imperial power.

During the Ming and Qing periods, the loong was widely used in architecture, porcelains, embroidery, and other areas of social life. Ming Dynasty scholars compiled the story of "Nine Sons of the Loong", naming all kinds of loong-shaped mythical creatures and giving them the identity of loong's offspring, which enriched the connotation of loong culture. In the middle and late Ming Dynasty, the front face of a loong pattern appeared, which became a royal pattern design. It is not only a simple decoration but also a cultural and political symbol, representing the supremacy of the imperial power and reflecting the social hierarchy. The Qing Dynasty continued to use this insignia-style loong pattern. Such exquisite five-clawed golden loong was usually decorated on the robe, chair, and bed as the exclusive symbol of the emperor, representing power and majesty. Loong culture also strikes root in people's hearts with various folk customs, such as loong lantern dances and loong boat races. These activities have become an important way of celebrating festivals and praying for good luck and have been passed down to the present day.

Connotation and Significance of the Loong Image

Significance of Religious Belief

From the origin of the loong image 8,000 years ago, the loong may have initially been associated with primitive religious beliefs. The people during the Middle Neolithic period regarded the loong as a being with supernatural power who could control natural elements such as wind and rain, mountains, and rivers. In ritual activities, the loong image may have served as a medium for communicating between humans and the gods, and people prayed for blessings and gifts from the gods through worshiping and sacrificing to the loong. Over time, loongs have played different roles in the religious belief systems of different cultural periods but have always been an important element associated with deities and ancestor worship.

Symbol of Political Power

The connection between loong and political power has gradually strengthened throughout historical development. Starting from the Hongshan culture, where the jade loong may have symbolized the power of the upper echelons of society, to the Shang and Zhou periods, when loong motifs embodied the kingship on bronzes, and then to the Qin and Han periods, when the loong became a symbol of imperial power, the symbolism of the loong in the political realm became increasingly explicit. Rulers associated the loong with their own identity, reinforcing their ruling authority through the image of the loong and making the people fearful of their power. This connotation of the loong as a symbol of political power continued and intensified during the feudal dynasty.

Symbol of Culture and National Spirit

The loong culture has occurred throughout the long history of the Chinese nation and has become an important symbol of the culture and national spirit of the Chinese nation. The meanings of good fortune, authority, and power represented by the loong reflect the Chinese people's aspiration and pursuit of a better life and their pride and sense of identity with their own nation. Loong culture integrates the Chinese nation's ideologies, beliefs, and values from various historical periods. It has a vast influence in various fields, such as literature, art, and folklore, greatly enhancing the cohesion of the Chinese nation.

By generalizing the loong images of artifacts found in archaeological discoveries from the Neolithic Age to the Ming and Qing Dynasties, we can clearly understand the progress of profound Chinese loong culture, which has gradually developed from a simple symbol of primitive worship into an important sign of political power, religious beliefs, and national spirituality. Over the past 8,000 years, loong culture has been developed and carried forward with its unique charm and has played an immeasurable role in the Chinese nation's formation, development, and cultural inheritance. As the totem of the Chinese nation, the loong fully embodies the outstanding consistency, originality, unity, inclusiveness, and peaceful nature of Chinese civilization. It is not only a treasure of the history and culture of the Chinese nation but also an important symbol of the unique identity of the Chinese nation in the world culture.

Chinese Archaeological Museum

January 5, 2025

《易经·乾卦》提到"见龙在田""飞龙在天"等卦辞。《陋室铭》有"水不在深，有龙则灵"。《说文解字·龙部》解释："龙，鳞虫之长，能幽能明，能细能巨，能短能长。春分而登天，秋分而潜渊。"历史文献中的龙神秘莫测，让人难辨其形；而考古发掘出土的众多龙形文物，构建出中国8000年龙文化的悠久历史。从史前到历史时期，中国龙文化的起源、形成和发展走过了多元一体的路径，随着龙文化的内涵日渐明确，龙的形象日渐统一，龙成为中华民族的图腾。

从考古发现看，新石器时代的中国龙形象与龙崇拜是多点起源。龙形象的来源主要包括以下几个方面：

一是各种动物，其中，以熊、野猪、鳄、蛇、鹿、虎、马和鹰为主；

二是动物胚胎，象征生命流转、物阜民康、子孙繁盛；

三是自然现象，包括风云闪电、彩虹、星象等，其中星象最为重要。

在新石器时代中期，随着农业生产和定居方式的成熟，龙的形象应运而生，先民将其视为图腾。辽宁阜新查海遗址出土了一条石堆龙，距今约8000年，这是目前通过科学考古发掘揭示出的中国最早的龙形象。这条石堆龙通长19.7米，由大小均匀的红褐色石块有规律地在聚落中部的广场堆砌而成，具有明显的祭祀功能，是中国8000年龙文化的开端。

中国农业起源可追溯至万年前，进入仰韶时代和龙山时代，南稻北粟的农业形态业已形成。农作物播种的时机是否准确决定了收成的丰歉，观象授时在农耕文化中尤为重要，作为星象的龙与农时产生了密切联系。

内蒙古敖汉旗小山遗址出土一件赵宝沟文化陶尊形器，其年代为距今约6800年，器腹外壁刻划有猪首蛇身的龙形象。中国是世界上最早驯化猪的国家之一，猪在现实世界是重要的动物资源，也是财富和权力的象征。此外，猪在后世曾是北斗的象征，《春秋说题辞》载"斗星时散精为彘"，而北斗是可以观象授时的星象。远古先民视蛇为神秘的动物，蛇蜕皮被看成是重生的表现。因此，远古先民在最初创造龙时借用了猪和蛇的形象。

辽宁阜新查海遗址石堆龙
（辽宁省文物考古研究院供图）

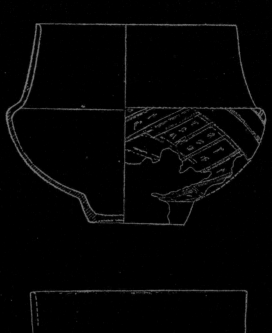

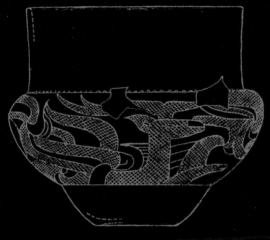

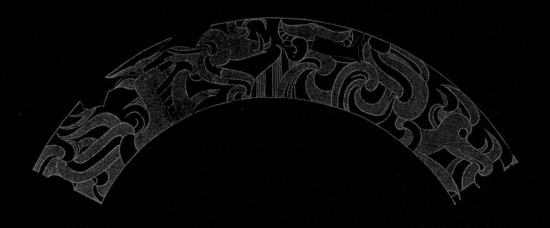

陶尊形器（85MAXIVF2②：30）

时　　代：新石器时代赵宝沟文化
　　　　　（距今约 7000—6400 年）
尺　　寸：高 25.5、口径 25.5 厘米
出土地点：内蒙古敖汉旗小山遗址
现 藏 地：中国考古博物馆

Pottery *Zun*
Neolithic Age Zhaobaogou Culture
(ca. 7000BP-6400BP)
Height 25.5 cm, mouth diameter 25.5 cm
Excavated from Xiaoshan site, Aohan Banner,
Inner Mongolia Autonomous Region
Chinese Archaeological Museum

　　磨光夹砂陶，高领直立，弧腹鼓肩，下接一凹底假圈足，腹部以网格纹填充空白处，等距刻划鹿首、鸟首、猪首的形象。鹿眼呈扁菱形，长角分叉、桃形耳。鸟圆眼，首上有冠，勾形长喙。猪眼细长，长吻前凸，獠牙竖立，身体遍饰鳞纹，卷曲如蛇。这是目前所知辽西地区最早的猪首龙形象。

河南濮阳西水坡遗址 M45 的墓主人和两侧蚌塑龙、虎
（资料来源：《濮阳西水坡》）

河南濮阳西水坡遗址出土有 3 组仰韶文化中期的蚌塑，均为淡水蚌壳，其年代为距今 6500—6300 年，其中一组摆放成龙、虎图案。有的研究者认为这条蚌塑龙比较接近鳄鱼的形象；也有的研究者认为这是中国最早的星象图，龙和虎的方位与四象中的东宫苍龙和西宫白虎相对应。

据学者研究，龙的形象最初可能和心宿三星产生联系，最终由东宫苍龙六宿所构成的图像作为代表。古人根据东宫苍龙的运转来确定四时轮回，所谓的"二月二，龙抬头"就是初春时节，黄昏时分，代表龙角的角宿出现在地平线上，之后不久，"见龙在田"，开始春耕。四时周而复始，轮回有序，"至信如时"，先民们把"信"作为道德最核心的内涵，从而建立起文明。

河南濮阳西水坡遗址 M45 蚌塑龙
（资料来源：《濮阳西水坡》）

河南濮阳西水坡遗址 M45 平、剖面图
（资料来源：《濮阳西水坡》）

2023 年 8 月，考古工作者在内蒙古自治区赤峰市松山区彩陶坡遗址发现了 1 件由蚌壳制作而成的龙，这是目前最新考古发现的红山文化早期的龙，其年代为距今约 6300 年，丰富了我国新石器时代龙的形象。

【红山文化】

　　红山文化因内蒙古赤峰市红山后遗址的发掘而得名，是中国东北地区最著名的新石器时代考古学文化之一，其年代为距今6500—5000年。红山文化玉龙分为玉"C"形龙和玉猪龙两大类，以玉猪龙的数量居多，应为部落首领或祭司的随身佩器。1984年，考古工作者在辽宁朝阳牛河梁遗址第二地点 M4 内发掘出土一对玉猪龙，这是首次通过正式科学考古发掘出土的红山文化玉猪龙，对研究龙的起源及崇龙礼俗的形成具有里程碑意义。

▲ 牛河梁遗址第二地点 M4 及玉器出土情况
［资料来源：《牛河梁——红山文化遗址发掘报告
（1983—2003 年度）》］

▼ 牛河梁遗址第二地点 M4 玉猪龙出土情况
［资料来源：《牛河梁——红山文化遗址发掘报告
（1983—2003 年度）》］

玉猪龙（N2Z1M4：2）

时　　代：新石器时代红山文化
　　　　　（距今约 6500—5000 年）
尺　　寸：通高 7.3、宽 5.6 厘米
出土地点：辽宁朝阳牛河梁遗址
现 藏 地：辽宁省文物考古研究院

Jade Coiled Loong
Neolithic Age Hongshan Culture
(ca. 6500BP-5000BP)
Height 7.3 cm, width 5.6 cm
Excavated from Niuheliang site, Chaoyang, Liaoning Province
Liaoning Provincial Institute of Cultural Relics and Archaeology

　　黄绿色玉，背、底部有红褐色斑沁，圆润光滑。兽首，玦形身。双耳呈尖弧状竖起，双目圆睁，吻部微凸，嘴巴略张，额顶施纹，龙体扁圆厚重，卷曲如环，首尾分割似玦，中部镂空，环孔表面平滑润泽。耳处有裂纹，背上部对钻一小孔，孔缘呈不规则圆形，造型手法细腻写实。出于墓主人胸部，墓主人为成年男性，同墓出土随葬器物共三件，两件玉猪龙及一件斜口筒形玉器。

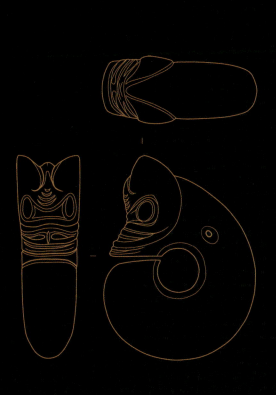

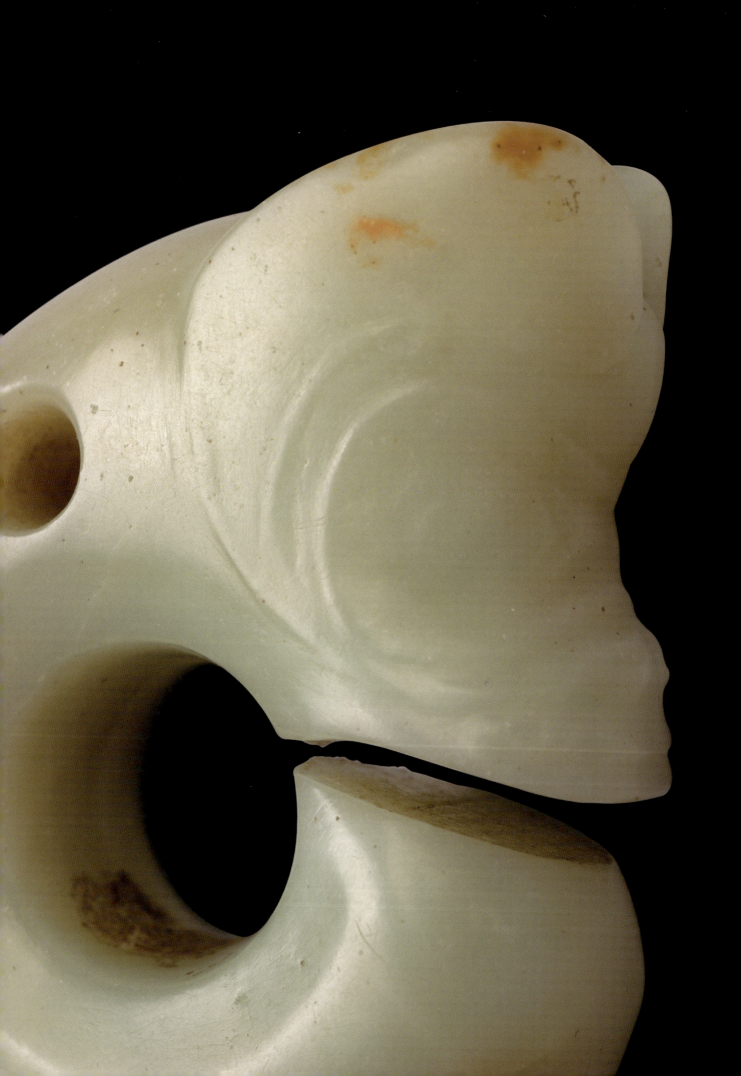

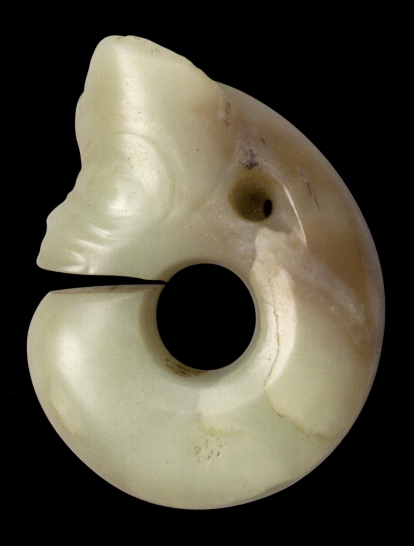

玉猪龙

时　　代：新石器时代红山文化
　　　　　（距今约 6500—5000 年）
尺　　寸：高 7.1、宽 5.9、厚 2.1 厘米
出土地点：内蒙古敖汉旗河西遗址
现 藏 地：敖汉博物馆

Jade Coiled Loong
Neolithic Age Hongshan Culture
(ca. 6500BP-5000BP)
Height 7.1 cm, width 5.9 cm, thickness 2.1 cm
Excavated from Hexi site, Aohan Banner, Inner Mongolia
Autonomous Region
Aohan Museum

　　黄绿色，有红褐色斑沁，通体抛光。兽首，头部较大，
双耳呈圆弧状竖起，双耳至顶部有一道棱脊。前额微凸，
圆目，菱形凸睛，吻部前伸，身体卷曲。颈部小孔对穿，
有磨损痕。中部大孔，孔壁抛光，孔缘起棱。缺口有
切割痕。

玉猪龙

时　　代：新石器时代红山文化
　　　　　（距今约 6500—5000 年）
尺　　寸：高 5.1、宽 5、厚 2.6 厘米
出土地点：内蒙古敖汉旗大五家村西
现 藏 地：敖汉博物馆

Jade Coiled Loong
Neolithic Age Hongshan Culture
(ca. 6500BP-5000BP)
Height 5.1 cm, width 5 cm, thickness 2.6 cm
Excavated from West Dawujia, Aohan Banner, Inner Mongolia
Autonomous Region
Aohan Museum

　　淡绿色，夹杂白色斑点并显露表皮，通体抛光。
兽首、块形身。双耳后扬、耳尖部磨平。前额略凸，
圆目，吻部前伸，身体卷曲。器体中部较大圆孔和
颈部偏上小孔均自两面对钻而成。

玉猪龙

时　　代：新石器时代红山文化
　　　　　（距今约 6500—5000 年）
尺　　寸：高 16.6、宽 10.8、厚 2.9 厘米
出土地点：内蒙古巴林右旗额尔根勿苏遗址
现 藏 地：巴林右旗博物馆

Jade Coiled Loong
Neolithic Age Hongshan Culture
(ca. 6500BP-5000BP)
Height 16.6 cm, width 10.8 cm, thickness 2.9 cm
Excavated from E'ergen Wusu site, Bairin Right Banner, Inner
Mongolia Autonomous Region
Bairin Right Banner Museum

　　墨绿色，夹杂黄褐色斑点。头部似猪首，立耳，圆眼，猪嘴，整体似猪的胚胎。器体中部较大圆孔和颈部偏上小孔均自两面对钻而成。玉猪龙是红山文化的代表器物，器身有穿孔，可能用于系绳佩挂。

玉"C"形龙

时　　代：新石器时代红山文化
　　　　　　（距今约6500—5000年）
尺　　寸：高16.7、身宽2.6、身厚1.8厘米
出土地点：翁牛特旗乌丹镇新地村东拐棒沟自然村
现 藏 地：翁牛特旗博物馆

C-shaped Jade Loong

Neolithic Age Hongshan Culture

(ca. 6500BP-5000BP)

Height 16.7 cm, body width 2.6 cm, body thickness 1.8 cm

Excavated from Dongguaibanggou Village, Xindi Village, Wudan
Town, Ongniud Banner, Inner Mongolia Autonomous Region

Ongniud Banner Museum

黄色玉，质地细腻温润，半透明，圆雕。身体卷曲呈"C"字形，吻部前伸且上翘，嘴巴紧闭，双目凸起呈棱形。颈脊竖起一道较短的片状勾角。下颌底部刻划疏朗的三角状纹。首尾分开。器体中部略偏上有一个两面对钻而成的小圆孔。此器造型生动、制作精良，是新石器时代红山玉龙成熟的代表。

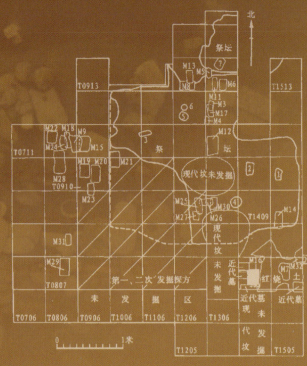

凌家滩第三次发掘（1998）探方平面图
（资料来源：《安徽含山县凌家滩遗址第三次发掘简报》）

【凌家滩文化】

　　凌家滩文化因安徽含山凌家滩遗址的发掘而得名，其年代为距今5800—5300年。1998年，考古工作者在凌家滩遗址M16内发现一件玉龙，身体呈环形，首尾相连，头顶部有双角，背部起脊，脊上刻均匀短斜线纹，靠近尾端有一小孔，其造型特征，与红山文化玉猪龙有别。2022年，考古工作者在凌家滩遗址新发现一件玉龙首形器，头部似猪首，与红山文化玉猪龙有相近之处，但其尾端呈尖状。此类造型的玉器在凌家滩文化中系首次发现，为中国龙文化起源和早期发展研究提供了最新考古实证。

安徽含山凌家滩遗址 M23 全景
（资料来源：《大酋长之墓——含山凌家滩 07M23 墓文化内涵试析》）

　　凌家滩遗址 M23 共有随葬品 330 件，其中玉器有 200 余件，是目前所知凌家滩遗址中出土玉器数量最多的一座大型墓葬。更为重要的是该墓内随葬一件大型玉猪，重达 88 千克，是迄今中国考古发现体积最大、体重最重、年代最早的透闪石玉猪，与红山文化玉猪龙、凌家滩文化玉龙首形器有紧密的内在联系。

玉猪（07 临 T1 ③：5）

时　　代：新石器时代凌家滩文化
　　　　　（距今约 5800—5300 年）
尺　　寸：长 72、宽 32 厘米
出土地点：安徽含山凌家滩遗址
现 藏 地：安徽博物院

Jade Boar
Neolithic Age Lingjiatan Culture
(ca. 5800BP-5300BP)
Length 72 cm, width 32 cm
Excavated from Lingjiatan site, Hanshan, Anhui Province
Anhui Museum

以透闪石为料，利用玉料的自然形态雕刻而成。双耳向上竖立，眼睛用减地法表现，吻部凸出，嘴部雕刻明显，其上有两个鼻孔，嘴两侧刻有向上弯曲的一对长獠牙。颈部呈半圆形，较宽且浅。腹部两侧简单琢出两条弯曲的线，形似双腿或翅膀。从颈部至尾部皆保留玉料原貌，无人为加工痕迹。

玉龙（98M16：2）

时　　代：新石器时代凌家滩文化
　　　　　（距今约 5800—5300 年）
尺　　寸：长径 4.4、短径 3.9、厚 0.2 厘米
出土地点：安徽含山凌家滩遗址
现 藏 地：含山博物馆

Jade Loong
Neolithic Age Lingjiatan Culture
(ca. 5800BP-5300BP)
Large diameter 4.4 cm, small diameter 3.9 cm, thickness 0.2 cm
Excavated from Lingjiatan site, Hanshan, Anhui Province
Hanshan Museum

灰白色泛青。表面琢磨光滑。呈椭圆形，较扁。龙首尾相连，吻部凸出，头顶雕刻两角，阴刻嘴、鼻、眼，脸部阴刻线条表现褶皱和龙须。龙身脊背阴刻规整圆弧线，连着弧线阴刻 17 条斜线并两面对刻，似龙身鳞片，靠近尾部有一对钻圆孔。玉龙两面雕刻基本相同，通体抛光，质地温润。

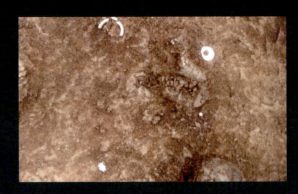

安徽含山凌家滩遗址玉龙出土情况
（资料来源：《凌家滩——田野考古发掘报告之一》）

玉龙首形器

时　代：新石器时代凌家滩文化
　　　　（距今约 5800—5300 年）
出土地点：安徽含山凌家滩遗址
现 藏 地：安徽省文物考古研究所

Jade Ware in the Shape of Loong Head
Neolithic Age Lingjiatan Culture
(ca. 5800BP-5300BP)
Excavated from Lingjiatan site, Hanshan, Anhui Province
Anhui Provincial Institute of Cultural Relics and Archaeology

　　玉龙首形器，造型奇特，工艺精湛，一端雕刻成猪龙首形，略上翘，另一端为尖锥形，是迄今我国史前考古发现的唯一一件玉龙首形器。

【良渚文化】

　　良渚文化因浙江余杭良渚遗址的发现而得名，其年代为距今 5300—4300 年，是长江下游环太湖流域最重要的新石器时代考古学文化之一。良渚文化玉器种类繁多，工艺精湛，具有极高的艺术价值，更能反映出良渚社会的权力结构、阶层分化及宗教信仰，是中华 5000 多年文明形成的重要标志。

有微凸的长吻、双眼和眼上部呈三角状向上凸出的双耳。眼底边缘有一道断续的近圆形阴刻线，似表示眼眶。

玉龙首饰（M17：2）

时　　代：新石器时代崧泽文化
　　　　　（距今约 6000—5300 年）
尺　　寸：高 1.2、宽 0.4、厚 1.1 厘米
出土地点：浙江桐乡普安桥遗址
现 藏 地：浙江省文物考古研究所

Jade Ornament in the Shape of Loong Head
Neolithic Age Songze Culture
(ca. 6000BP-5300BP)
Height 1.2 cm, width 0.4 cm, thickness 1.1 cm
Excavated from Pu'anqiao site, Tongxiang, Zhejiang Province
Zhejiang Provincial Institute of Cultural Relics and Archaeology

　　龙首，器形很小，呈不规则圆环状。一侧雕有微凸的长吻、双眼和眼上部呈三角状向上凸出的双耳。眼底边缘有一道断续的近圆形阴刻线，似表示眼眶。

玉龙首饰（M8：28）

时　　代：新石器时代崧泽文化
　　　　　（距今约6000—5300年）
尺　　寸：高3.1、宽1.3、厚1.6厘米
出土地点：浙江桐乡普安桥遗址
现 藏 地：浙江省文物考古研究所

Jade Ornament in the Shape of Loong Head
Neolithic Age Songze Culture
(ca. 6000BP-5300BP)
Height 3.1 cm, width 1.3 cm, thickness 1.6 cm
Excavated from Pu'anqiao site, Tongxiang, Zhejiang Province
Zhejiang Provincial Institute of Cultural Relics and Archaeology

　　玉质为白色，夹有紫褐色结晶斑，整体近似圆
柱体。龙首，器形较小，呈不规则椭圆形。头部呈
半圆雕状，正面浮雕龙首五官，口部向内切割1厘
米许后向上切割至眼角后侧。长吻，凸鼻。眼珠圆鼓，
底部边缘刻有眼眶线条，施刻椭圆形或菱形单线似
表示眼睛。横向立耳，凹凸弯弧明显。整体精心研磨，
表面不见切割痕迹。

玉龙首饰（M65：20）

时　代：新石器时代良渚文化
　　　　（距今约5300—4300年）
尺　寸：直径1.6、孔径0.6—0.7、厚0.55厘米
出土地点：浙江杭州官井头遗址
现 藏 地：浙江省文物考古研究所

Jade Ornament in the Shape of Loong Head
Neolithic Age Liangzhu Culture
(ca. 5300BP-4300BP)
Diameter 1.6 cm, hole diameter 0.6-0.7 cm, thickness 0.55 cm
Excavated from Guanjingtou site, Hangzhou, Zhejiang Province
Zhejiang Provincial Institute of Cultural Relics and Archaeology

　　乳白色，带浅灰色晶斑。环形，器物较小。外缘一侧雕琢有龙首形象，有犄角、双目和上翘的吻部，双眼为较小的圆形。外壁圆润，中部不等距双面钻孔。

玉龙首饰（M47 ∶ 9）

时　　代：新石器时代良渚文化
　　　　　（距今约5300—4300年）
尺　　寸：直径1.6、孔径0.4、厚0.6厘米
出土地点：浙江杭州官井头遗址
现 藏 地：浙江省文物考古研究所

Jade Ornament in the Shape of Loong Head
Neolithic Age Liangzhu Culture
(ca. 5300BP-4300BP)
Diameter 1.6 cm, hole diameter 0.4 cm, thickness 0.6 cm
Excavated from Guanjingtou site, Hangzhou, Zhejiang Province
Zhejiang Provincial Institute of Cultural Relics and Archaeology

　　青色玉。环形，器物较小。在一侧雕有龙首形象，长吻微凸，大半圆眼泡微鼓，眼泡上施刻内外双圈眼纹，双耳呈三角状凸出。

玉龙首镯（M106：50）

时　　代：新石器时代良渚文化
　　　　　（距今约 5300—4300 年）
尺　　寸：外径 7.7—8、内径 5.25、厚 0.8—1 厘米
出土地点：浙江余杭北村遗址
现 藏 地：浙江省文物考古研究所

Jade Bracelet with Loong Heads Design
Neolithic Age Liangzhu Culture
(ca. 5300BP-4300BP)
Outer diameter 7.7-8 cm, inner diameter 5.25 cm, thickness 0.8-1 cm
Excavated from Beicun site, Yuhang, Zhejiang Province
Zhejiang Provincial Institute of Cultural Relics and Archaeology

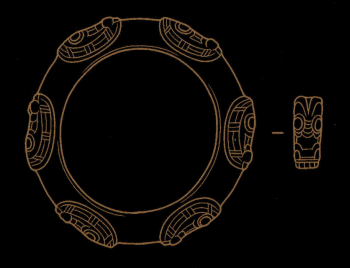

　　M106 为良渚文化早期的高等级贵族墓，该玉镯出土于墓主左手处。黄白色，圆环形。外壁琢刻凸面，以减地浅浮雕、阴刻线的方式等距离琢刻 6 个长 2.4—2.6 厘米的龙首纹，颇为罕见。龙首纹最显眼的部位为凸出的浅浮雕双角、圆形双眼和宽扁大嘴。刻划生动而传神，工艺高超，代表了良渚文化先民的崇龙礼俗与审美观念。

玉琮（瑶山 M9：4）

时　　代：新石器时代良渚文化
　　　　　（距今约 5300—4300 年）
尺　　寸：高 4.5、射径 7.95、内径 6.3 厘米
出土地点：浙江余杭瑶山遗址
现 藏 地：浙江省文物考古研究所

Jade Cong
Neolithic Age Liangzhu Culture
(ca. 5300BP-4300BP)
Height 4.5 cm, outer diameter 7.95 cm, inner diameter 6.3 cm
Excavated from Yaoshan site, Yuhang, Zhejiang Province
Zhejiang Provincial Institute of Cultural Relics and Archaeology

　　有灰褐色瑕斑。圆筒形，孔壁微凸，但经打磨。
器表有 4 个对称的长方形弧凸面，各饰一组神兽纹，
图案基本相同。椭圆形眼眶、额、嘴均为浅浮雕，
圆眼管钻而成。鼻微隆起，鼻翼阔，阴刻出鼻孔。
嘴扁宽且弧凸，上面阴线刻出两对獠牙。

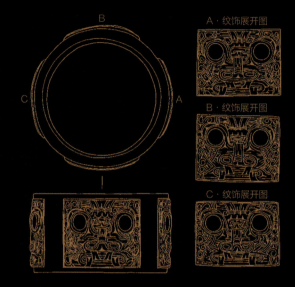

瑶山墓地出土玉琮线图
（资料来源：《瑶山》）

陶寺

【陶寺文化】

　　陶寺文化因山西襄汾陶寺遗址的发掘而得名，其年代为距今4300—3900年。在已发掘的墓葬中，有4座大墓中各出土1件陶彩绘龙纹盘，推测龙纹是以短腹蝮蛇为原型，该类陶盘应该为祭祀用器。鉴于陶寺文化处于比较发达的史前农业经济阶段，当时人种植的主要农作物包括粟、黍、稻和大豆等，推测龙口衔之物可能为农作物的穗，隐含着陶寺先民期盼农业丰收的美好愿望。

山西襄汾陶寺遗址陶彩绘龙纹盘出土情况
（资料来源：《襄汾陶寺——1978—1985年考古发掘报告》）

陶彩绘龙纹盘（JS62M3072：6）

时　　代：新石器时代陶寺文化
　　　　　（距今约 4300—3900 年）
尺　　寸：高 9.0、口径 37.0 厘米
出土地点：山西襄汾陶寺遗址
现 藏 地：中国考古博物馆

Painted Pottery Plate with Loong Design
Neolithic Age Taosi Culture
(ca. 4300BP-3900BP)
Height 9 cm, mouth diameter 37 cm
Excavated from Taosi site, Xiangfen, Shanxi Province
Chinese Archaeological Museum

　　出土于陶寺遗址大型墓内。胎褐色，器表深灰间灰褐色，内壁及盘心涂黑色陶衣并磨光。唇、沿面及内壁上缘涂红，内壁以黑陶衣为地，用红彩绘出龙纹，以底色表现龙的圆目，以红色与底色相间布置来表现龙躯的鳞片，尾部及盘心的圆形红彩已磨蚀不清。龙采用蛇身和鳄鱼头形象组合而成，由外向内盘绕，龙首位于陶盘的边沿处，头上有角，是目前我国发现的最早带有鳞片的龙形象。龙口中衔着谷物，说明龙与农业的关系，表明陶寺遗址处于比较发达的农业社会。盘腹外壁上段有绳纹，又经抹消。

山西襄汾陶寺遗址 M3072 平面及随葬器物组合图
（资料来源：《襄汾陶寺——1978—1985 年考古发掘报告》）

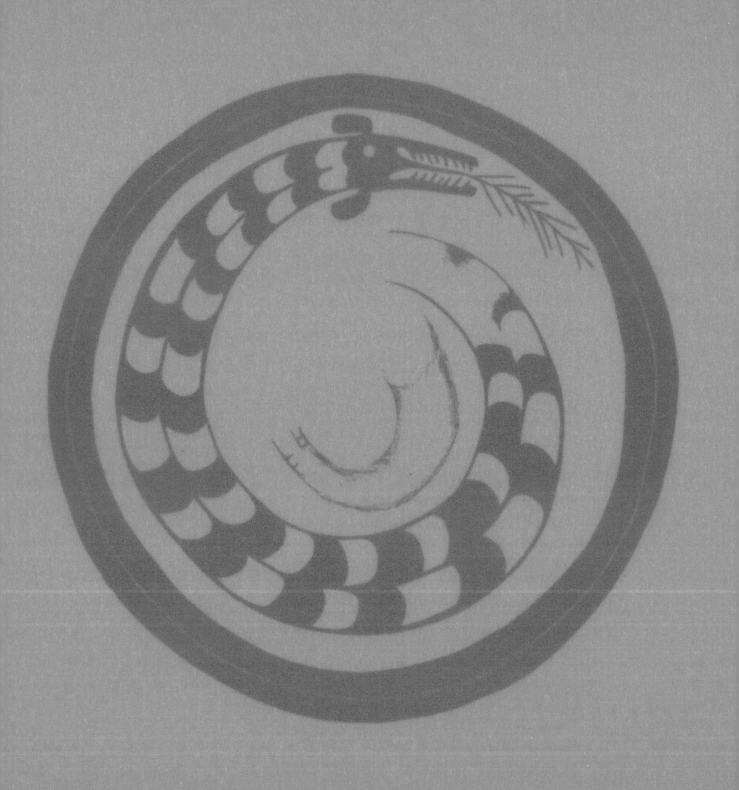

刻纹陶片（2022JXTIJ1）

时　　代：新石器时代陶寺文化
　　　　　（距今约 4300—3900 年）
尺　　寸：长 8.5、宽 2.1—2.5 厘米
出土地点：山西襄汾陶寺遗址
现 藏 地：中国考古博物馆

Incised Pottery Sherd
Neolithic Age Taosi Culture
(ca. 4300BP-3900BP)
Length 8.5 cm, width 2.1-2.5 cm
Excavated from Taosi site, Xiangfen, Shanxi Province
Chinese Archaeological Museum

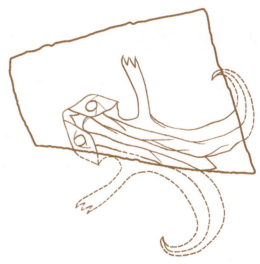

刻划纹复原图
（资料来源：《试析陶寺遗址 2022JXTIJ1 出土动物形
刻划纹饰》）

　　泥质灰陶，器表线刻兽面纹样，阔脸，"臣"
字目，蒜头鼻。从陶寺文化至新砦文化，再至二里
头文化，乃至商周时期，一些龙蛇形象尤其一首
双身龙似乎存在着一定程度的文化形象上的认同、
吸收、融合、改造并传承的内在嬗变关系，陶寺
的这类动物形象极有可能是夏商周龙纹的重要来
源之一。

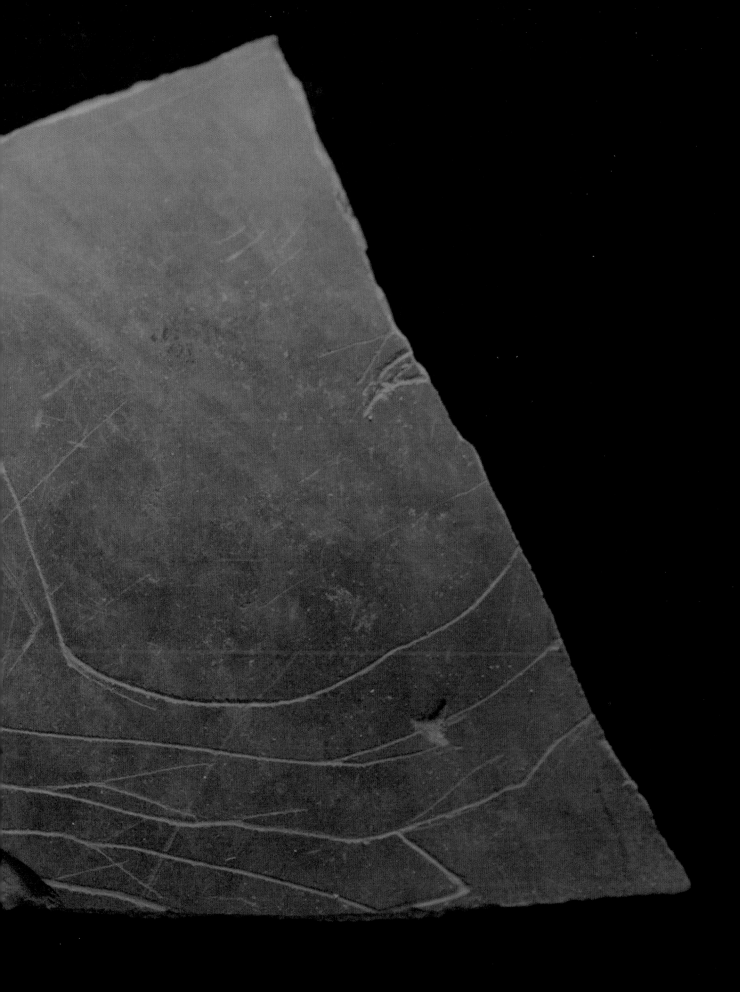

第二篇章

龙行天下

夏商周时期，中国早期文明从"多元"凝聚为"一体"，特征统一的龙形象大量出现在高规格、高等级的墓葬中和器物上。龙的形象融入了鹿角、虎头和鸟爪，强调了蛇身，使得龙"潜渊"和"登天"的意义更加明确。甲骨文和金文中的"龙"字和龙的形象达成一致。春秋时期，吸纳中原文化的牧业人群对龙的形象进行了创新并传播到更为广阔的地区。战国时期，龙为东方之象，正式位列四象，即苍龙、白虎、朱雀和玄武。四象的理念在东亚地区广受重视。

【 新砦文化 】

　　新砦文化因河南新密新砦遗址的发掘而得名，其年代为距今 3800—3700 年。经过历年的考古发掘，现已基本确认新砦遗址是一处由内壕、城壕和外壕构成的具有三重环壕的大型都邑性城址，根据相关文献记载，结合考古研究，初步推测新砦遗址为"夏启之居"，即夏王朝夏启都城所在地。遗址中出土 1 件陶器盖残片上阴刻有龙纹，方头和"臣"字目的形态与二里头遗址出土的绿松石龙有相似之处，应为其最直接的渊源或祖型，成为探索早期夏文化的重要线索。

刻纹陶器盖残片（1999T1H24：1）

时　　代：新砦文化
　　　　　（距今约3800—3700年）
尺　　寸：残长9.3、宽3.1—5.6厘米
出土地点：河南新密新砦遗址
现 藏 地：郑州市文物考古研究院

Incised Pottery Lid Sherd
Xinzhai Culture
(ca. 3800BP-3700BP)
Length 9.3 cm, width 3.1-5.6 cm
Excavated from Xinzhai site, Xinmi, Henan Province
Zhengzhou Municipal Institute of Archaeology

泥质陶，外表涂黑衣，器表磨光，以双阴线刻划出龙纹，仅残存龙首大部分和龙尾一角。龙首主体近方圆形，"臣"字形纵目，蒜头鼻，长条形鼻梁，鼻梁上刻四条两组平行阴线，将鼻梁分为三节。吻部略前凸，两侧有双阴线内弯。龙首纹样与二里头遗址出土的绿松石龙形象较一致，表明二者具有较为密切的关系。

【二里头文化】

　　河南偃师二里头遗址出土的龙形象有陶塑、雕刻、绿松石粘嵌三大类，属于二里头文化，其年代为距今 3800—3500 年。二里头绿松石龙形器是由 2000 余片绿松石嵌片组合而成，原应粘嵌在某种有机物上，上面还有一枚铜铃。这件龙形器被放置于墓主的身上，呈拥揽状态。该龙形器用工之巨、制作之精、体量之大，在中国龙文化发展史上十分罕见，是夏代中晚期最具代表性的龙形象文物。

绿松石龙形器（2002 V M3 ∶ 5）

时　　代：二里头文化
　　　　　（距今约 3800—3500 年）
尺　　寸：龙身长 64.5、整器长 70.3 厘米
出土地点：河南偃师二里头遗址
现 藏 地：中国考古博物馆

Turquoise-inlaid Loong

Erlitou Culture

(ca. 3800BP-3500BP)

Body length 64.5 cm, length 70.3 cm

Excavated from Erlitou site, Yanshi, Henan Province

Chinese Archaeological Museum

　　放置于墓主人骨架之上。由 2000 余片绿松石
组合而成，原应粘嵌在某种有机物上。巨头蜷尾。
龙头置于绿松石片粘嵌而成的近梯形托座上，为
扁圆形巨首，吻部略凸出。以三节青、白玉柱组
成额面中脊和鼻梁。眼睛为梭形，眼眶内嵌绿松
石片，以顶面弧凸的圆饼形白玉为睛。龙身中部
最宽处 4 厘米，龙身近尾部渐变为圆弧隆起，尾
尖内蜷。绿松石片象征鳞纹，遍布全身。龙尾端 3.6
厘米处，发现一件绿松石条形饰，与龙体近于垂直，
二者之间有红色漆痕相连。

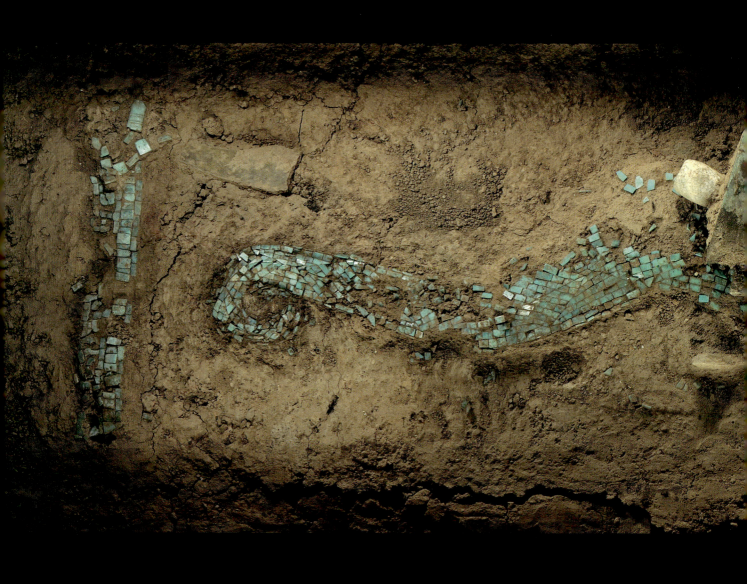

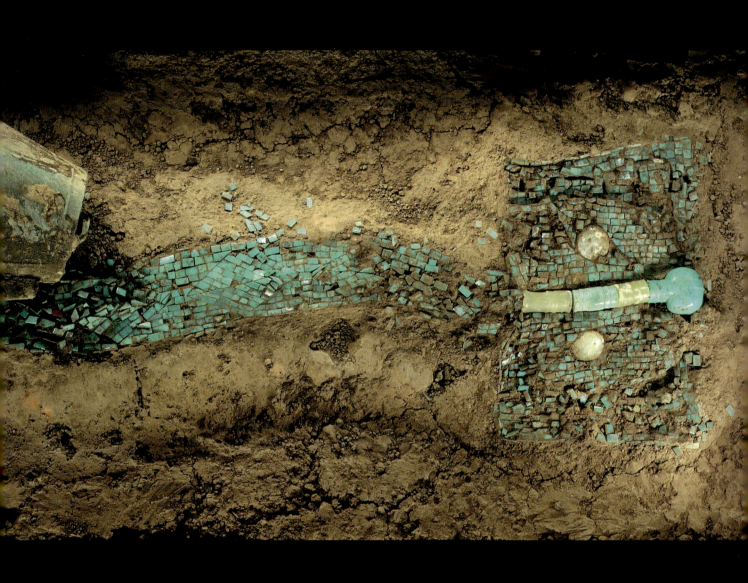

鱼龙纹大陶盆

时　　代：二里头文化
　　　　　（距今约 3800—3500 年）
尺　　寸：口径 63、高 19 厘米
出土地点：河南偃师二里头遗址
现　藏　地：中国考古博物馆

Pottery Basin with Fish and Loong　Design
Erlitou Culture
(ca. 3800BP-3500BP)
Mouth diameter 63 cm, height 19 cm
Excavated from Erlitou site, Yanshi, Henan Province
Chinese Archaeological Museum

泥质灰陶。大敞口，圆唇，卷沿，斜弧壁，平底。口沿外壁等距饰三条乳钉纹和凸棱的宽带状錾，腹及底部外壁饰数周凹弦纹及绳纹，口沿内壁刻划数条鱼纹，堆塑一周龙纹。

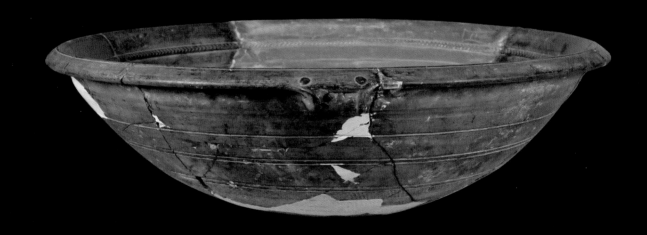

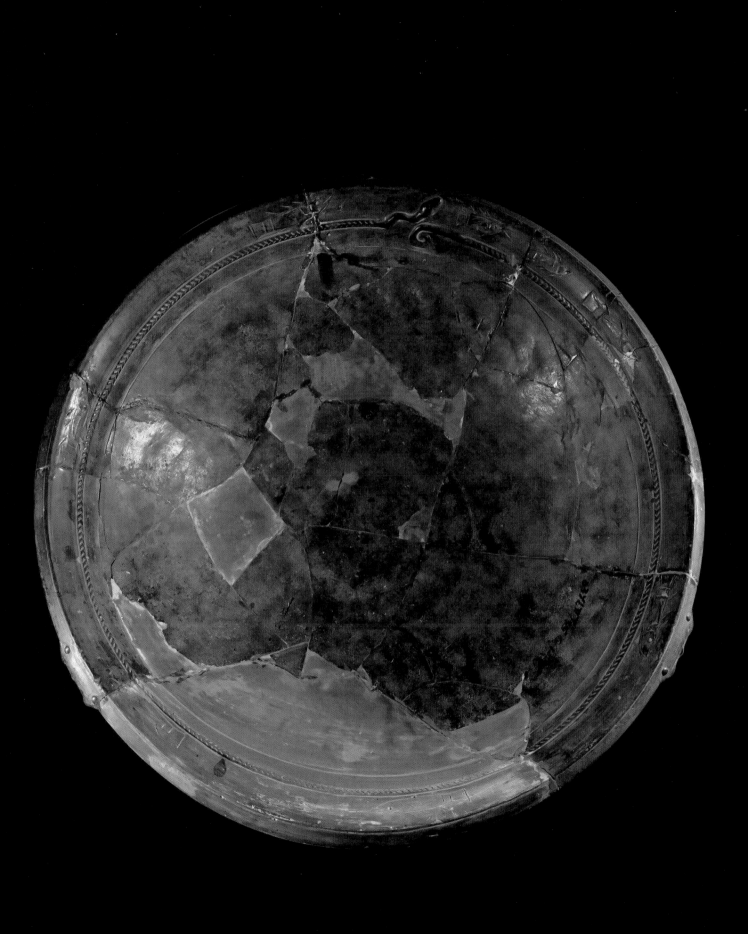

蛇纹鬲陶片（T2432 ⑤：3）

时　　代：夏家店下层文化
　　　　　（距今约 4000—3400 年）
尺　　寸：残长 12.01、宽 6.91、厚 0.89 厘米
出土地点：内蒙古敖汉旗西大梁遗址
现 藏 地：中国考古博物馆

Pottery Sherd of *Li* with Snake Design
Lower Xiajiadian Culture
(ca. 4000BP-3400BP)
Length 12.01 cm, width 6.91 cm, thickness 0.89 cm
Excavated from Xidaliang site, Aohan Banner,
Inner Mongolia Autonomous Region
Chinese Archaeological Museum

泥质灰陶，为陶鬲领下及上腹部残片。外壁施浅而密的细绳纹，其上贴塑有一道曲折如爬行之蛇的细泥条附加堆纹，堆纹上端略宽，两侧各有一道竖向的相互平行的细泥条附加堆纹。早期龙纹为多种动物组合而成，身体往往采用蛇的形态。

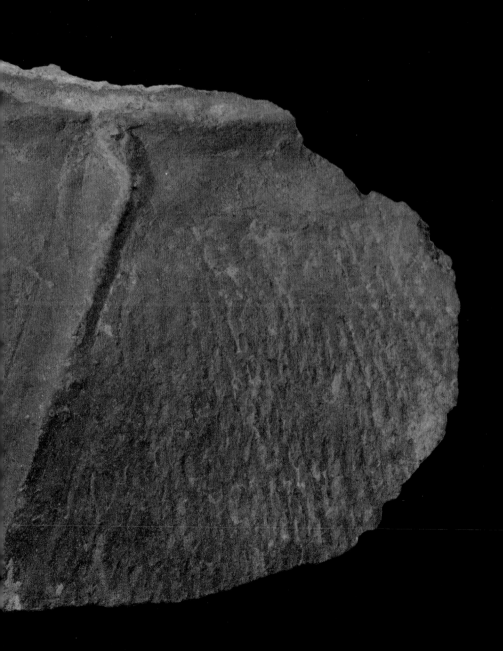

鳄鱼骨板（T2232④：2）

时　　代：夏家店下层文化
　　　　　（距今约 4000—3400 年）
尺　　寸：长 2.43、宽 3.11、厚 0.5 厘米
出土地点：内蒙古敖汉旗西大梁遗址
现 藏 地：中国考古博物馆

Alligator Lamella
Lower Xiajiadian Culture
(ca. 4000BP-3400BP)
Length 2.43 cm, width 3.11 cm, thickness 0.5 cm
Excavated from Xidaliang site, Aohan Banner, Inner Mongolia
Autonomous Region
Chinese Archaeological Museum

　　平面近方形，背面略内凹，正面有许多点状小坑，中
心凸起一条脊棱。鳄鱼骨板在龙山时期高等级墓葬中多有
发现，在山西襄汾陶寺遗址发现过用鳄鱼皮制成鼓面的鼍
鼓，均出土于大型墓中，成为贵族身份地位的特有标志物。
鳄鱼也是新石器时代龙形象的来源之一。

【商代】

　　商代，龙的种类和数量显著增多，从造型特征看，蜷体、有角和凸出背脊等特征明显受到红山文化、凌家滩文化的影响。良渚文化"神人兽面纹"的面部构图和沿袭陶寺文化、二里头文化的马蹄形、菱形格状的龙鳞在商代龙纹上浑然一体，是中国龙文化多元一体发展历程的重要体现。至商代晚期，龙纹风格从简单质朴逐渐转向庄重华丽，龙的造型也随之多样化，成为商代青铜器和玉器上最常见、最显著的主题，体现了商代敬天法地的祭祀礼仪和宗教信仰。

甲骨文和金文中的"龙"字同龙的形象以及"东宫苍龙"星象达成一致。

龍

龍

龍

龍

龍

龍

殷墟

【 妇好墓 】

　　妇好墓是1976年在河南安阳殷墟发现的目前唯一保存完整的商代王室墓。墓中出土的青铜器、玉器、宝石器等，为我们深入了解商代后期历史文化提供了重要资料。墓上享堂被称为"母辛宗"，是为了祭祀妇好而专门建造的宗庙建筑。墓中出土了众多与龙相关的精美文物，充分展示了商代晚期对龙的崇拜和艺术表现特点。

《诗·商颂·玄鸟》："天命玄鸟，降而生商……龙旂十乘，大糦是承。"
《诗·商颂·长发》："有娀方将，帝立子生商。"
《史记·殷本纪》："殷契，母曰简狄，有娀氏之女，为帝喾次妃。三人行浴，见玄鸟堕其卵，简狄取吞之，因孕生契。"

妇好圈足铜觥（1976AXTM5：802）

时　　代：商代晚期
尺　　寸：通高 22.0、通长 28.4 厘米
出土地点：河南安阳殷墟妇好墓
现 藏 地：中国考古博物馆

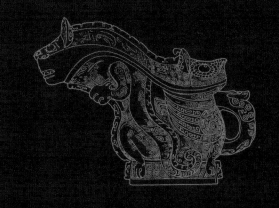

Fuhao Bronze *Gong* with Ring Foot
Late Shang
Height 22 cm, length 28.4 cm
Excavated from Fuhao Tomb, Ruins of Yin, Anyang, Henan Province
Chinese Archaeological Museum

　　妇好墓出土铜觥 8 件，有圈足和四足两种形制。此觥盖首作虎形，张口露齿，两耳竖起；盖尾作鸮形，尖喙圆眼，竖耳。盖中部有一条长扁棱，两端与虎首和鸮首相连，棱两侧饰夔纹。盖下周沿有子口，与器身口相衔接。器身短流，扁长体，扁圆形矮圈足，底略外鼓，牛首鋬，流下有细棱，下通圈足，圈足后端亦有一条短棱。底里中部铸有阴文铭文"妇好"二字。器物设计极为巧妙，器盖相合后，前端如一蹲坐状的虎，虎前肢抱颈，后肢作蹲状，长尾上卷；后端为一站立状的鸮，双翅并拢，爪着地。

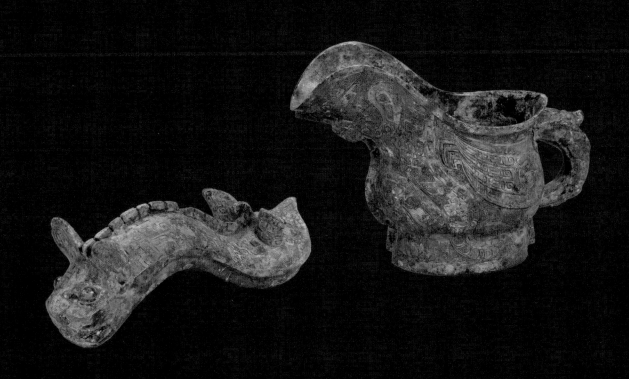

铜圆斝（1976AXTM5：861）

时　　代：商代晚期
尺　　寸：通高 61.8、口径 29.2 厘米
出土地点：河南安阳殷墟妇好墓
现 藏 地：中国考古博物馆

Bronze Round *Jia*
Late Shang
Height 61.8 cm, mouth diameter 29.2 cm
Excavated from Fuhao Tomb, Ruins of Yin,
Anyang, Henan Province
Chinese Archaeological Museum

侈口，厚唇，口沿上对称直立一对伞形立柱，柱上有细棱。柱伞表面饰圆涡纹和三角纹，下饰云雷纹，环柱一周，口沿下饰三角纹。腹分上下两段，束腰，底近平。上下腹面均饰饕餮纹，以扉棱为鼻梁，饕餮两侧均饰有倒夔纹和云雷纹，足面饰对夔蕉叶纹。腹上铸一兽首鋬手，与两立柱垂直一侧，兽首上立两只大耳，双眼圆睁。腹底铸实心扁形足三组，足底端外撇。腹底内里中部有铭文"其"一字，应是方国名或族名。

铜圆斝（1976AXTM5：781）

时　　代：商代晚期
尺　　寸：通高 48.4、口径 22.3 厘米
出土地点：河南安阳殷墟妇好墓
现 藏 地：中国考古博物馆

Bronze Round *Jia*
Late Shang
Height 48.4 cm, mouth diameter 22.3 cm
Excavated from Fuhao Tomb, Ruins of Yin, Anyang,
Henan Province
Chinese Archaeological Museum

　　侈口，厚唇，口沿上对称直立一对伞形立柱，
柱上有细棱。柱伞表面饰圆涡纹和三角纹，下饰云
雷纹，环柱一周，口沿下饰三角纹。腹分上下两段，
束腰，底近平。上下腹面均饰饕餮纹，以扉棱为鼻梁，
饕餮两侧均饰有倒夔纹和云雷纹，足面饰对夔蕉叶
纹。腹上铸一兽首鋬手，与两立柱垂直一侧，双眼
圆睁。

妇好铜封口盉（1976AXTM5：859）

时　　代：商代晚期
尺　　寸：通高 38.4 厘米
出土地点：河南安阳殷墟妇好墓
现 藏 地：中国考古博物馆

Fuhao Bronze *He* with Sealed Mouth
Late Shang
Height 38.4 cm
Excavated from Fuhao Tomb, Ruins of Yin, Anyang,
Henan Province
Chinese Archaeological Museum

封口，顶面隆起弧形，边沿较宽平，前端有一斜立的筒形流，后端开一长方形小口。颈部内收，下体如鬲，分裆款足，实心足跟。口下有牛头空心鋬。顶面饰饕餮纹，眉眼清楚，以器口作饕餮的口，在饕餮的后端两侧各饰一夔，颈饰斜角云雷纹，腹饰阴线大饕餮纹三组，流上端饰饕餮纹两组，其下饰三角形纹四个。鋬内壁面有"妇好"二字，但不甚清晰。

122

铜龙首提梁卣（1976AXTM5：765）

时　　代：商代晚期
尺　　寸：通高 36.4、口径 8.8 厘米
出土地点：河南安阳殷墟妇好墓
现 藏 地：中国考古博物馆

Bronze *You* with Swing-handle in the Shape of Loong Head
Late Shang
Height 36.4 cm, mouth diameter 8.8 cm
Excavated from Fuhao Tomb, Ruins of Yin, Anyang, Henan Province
Chinese Archaeological Museum

　　盛酒器，由器盖、器身和提梁三部分组成。盖面呈弧形，中部铸有一鸟，以作盖钮。在盖面上有一附加的活动环带，环带由一盘卷状的夔和一鸟所构成，鸟尾作成小环形，与提梁内侧的小环相套合，启盖后，盖可悬于梁。盖面边缘饰雷纹一周。盖下周沿有内折的子口，与器口相合。小口，细长颈，鼓腹圆底，矮直圈足，圈足上有对称长方形小穿，颈、腹、足两面均有一条细扉棱。腹部有对称的小环钮，其上安有龙首提梁，梁面正中有　条细棱脊，与两端的龙首相连。提梁两端铸龙首与器身相连，两龙共用一体，设计精巧。口下饰一周雷纹，颈、腹、圈足均饰饕餮纹，口都向下，铸纹细浅，大部分锈蚀不清。

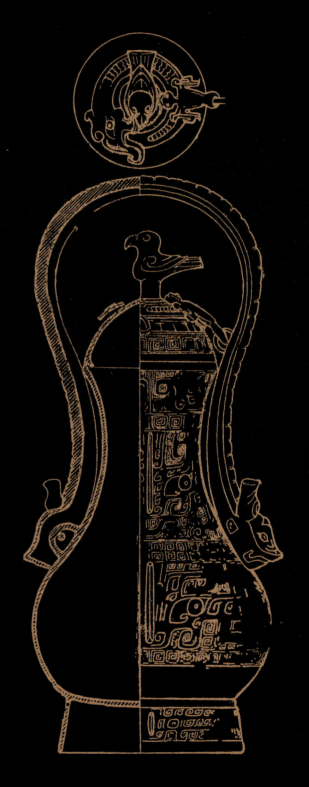

铜龙首提梁卣（1977AXTM18：10）

时　　代：商代晚期
尺　　寸：高28、腹径13.6厘米
出土地点：河南安阳殷墟遗址
现 藏 地：中国考古博物馆

Bronze *You* with Swing-handle in the Shape of Loong Head
Late Shang
Height 28 cm, belly diameter 13.6 cm
Excavated from Ruins of Yin, Anyang, Henan Province
Chinese Archaeological Museum

盛酒器，由器盖、器身和提梁三部分组成。盖呈弧形，上有菌状钮，下部周缘有内折子口，与器口相合。盖周饰云雷纹一周，钮饰涡纹。小口外侈，颈细长，腹下部外鼓，腹两侧有环形钮。圈足直矮，上有长方形小孔。颈饰凸弦纹两周，其下饰饕餮纹两组，大嘴，细窄鼻梁，"目"字形眼，眸子凸起，圈足饰雷纹一周。提梁整体呈双头龙造型，两端龙首下探，表面饰斜方格纹兼三角纹。龙首背面有横梁，与腹两侧半环形钮相套合。铜龙首提梁卣上的双龙首提梁与龙首玉璜一样，可能表达了彩虹式的双龙吸水意象。

陶范（2003AXST2007⑥：9）

时　　代：商代晚期
尺　　寸：长 10.6、宽 7.2 厘米
出土地点：河南安阳殷墟遗址
现 藏 地：中国考古博物馆

Pottery Mould
Late Shang
Length 10.6 cm, width 7.2 cm
Excavated from Ruins of Yin, Anyang, Henan Province
Chinese Archaeological Museum

为鼎范的口和上腹部范，较完整。面范泥质，背范夹粗砂，青灰色，分层线明显。上分型面有二榫，左右分型面各有一卯，下分型面有二卯。饰夔纹，云雷纹衬地。此鼎范上腹部以扉棱垂直分为六扇，从上下腹部水平分为上下两段。

陶范（2003AXSH481③：1）

时　　代：商代晚期
尺　　寸：长12.6、宽11.5厘米
出土地点：河南安阳殷墟遗址
现 藏 地：中国考古博物馆

Pottery Mould
Late Shang
Length 12.6 cm, width 11.5 cm
Excavated from Ruins of Yin, Anyang, Henan Province
Chinese Archaeological Museum

　　为鼎范的耳、口和上腹部范。面范和背范均为泥质，青灰色，有分层线。立耳，耳部分型面上有二榫，腹部左右分型面各有一榫，下分型面有二卯。面范耳部饰两夔龙，夔首相对，上腹部以云雷纹衬地，饰鸟纹和兽面纹，有扉棱，花纹清晰精美。背面凹凸不平，有较多手指印痕，部分指印内残留少量砂质泥。此范在鼎上腹部水平分范，在上腹部扉棱处垂直分范。

妇好墓中共出土尺形器28件，其中龙首尺形器11件，可能是插嵌在漆木器上的装饰。

铜龙首尺形器（1976AXTM5：697）

时　　代：商代晚期
尺　　寸：通长 28、柄宽 2.2 厘米
出土地点：河南安阳殷墟妇好墓
现 藏 地：中国考古博物馆

Ruler-shaped Bronze Ware with Loong Head
Late Shang
Length 28 cm, handle width 2.2 cm
Excavated from Fuhao Tomb, Ruins of Yin, Anyang, Henan Province
Chinese Archaeological Museum

　　头端作龙形，"目"字形眼，独角竖立，唇下垂，短身卷尾，竖看似"冠"。在龙身的下侧有一倒夔，两者巧妙地合为一体。夔口衔扁平长条形柄，柄的下端较宽，厚钝无刃，上端饰云纹和三角形纹。

铜龙首尺形器（1976AXTM5：692）

时　　代：商代晚期
尺　　寸：通长 28、柄宽 2.5 厘米
出土地点：河南安阳殷墟妇好墓
现 藏 地：中国考古博物馆

Ruler-shaped Bronze Ware with Loong Head
Late Shang
Length 28 cm, handle width 2.5 cm
Excavated from Fuhao Tomb, Ruins of Yin, Anyang, Henan
Province
Chinese Archaeological Museum

　　龙首形饰，龙头作侧视相，结构完整，头端为
龙形，张嘴露齿，顶部为锯齿状，"目"字形眼，
独角竖立，唇下垂，短身卷尾，竖看似"冠"。在
龙身的下侧有一倒夔，两者巧妙地合为一体。夔口
衔扁平长条形柄，柄的下端较宽，厚钝无刃，上端
饰云纹和三角形纹，线条简练清晰。

铜龙首尺形器（1976AXTM5：695）

时　　代：商代晚期
尺　　寸：通长 27.5、柄宽 2.4 厘米
出土地点：河南安阳殷墟妇好墓
现 藏 地：中国考古博物馆

Ruler-shaped Bronze Ware with Loong Head
Late Shang
Length 27.5 cm, handle width 2.4 cm
Excavated from Fuhao Tomb, Ruins of Yin, Anyang, Henan
Province
Chinese Archaeological Museum

　　龙首形饰，龙头作侧视相，结构完整，头端为龙形，
"目"字形眼，独角竖立，唇下垂，短身卷尾，竖看
似"冠"。在龙身的下侧有一倒夔，两者巧妙地合为
一体。夔口衔扁平长条形柄，柄的下端较宽，厚钝无刃，
上端饰云纹和三角形纹，表面纹饰锈蚀严重。

铜龙首尺形器（1976AXTM5：1599）

时　　代：商代晚期
尺　　寸：通长 28、柄宽 2.5 厘米
出土地点：河南安阳殷墟妇好墓
现 藏 地：中国考古博物馆

Ruler-shaped Bronze Ware with Loong Head
Late Shang
Length 28 cm, handle width 2.5 cm
Excavated from Fuhao Tomb, Ruins of Yin, Anyang, Henan Province
Chinese Archaeological Museum

　　龙首形饰，龙头作侧视相，结构完整，头端为龙形，张嘴露齿，上颚二齿，下颚一齿，獠牙粗壮，顶部为锯齿状，圆眼，边缘凸起，"目"字形眼，独角竖立，唇下垂，短身卷尾，竖看似"冠"。在龙身的下侧有一倒夔，两者巧妙地合为一体。夔口衔扁平长条形柄，柄的下端较宽，厚钝无刃，上端饰云纹和三角形纹，线条简练清晰。

铜龙首尺形器（1976AXTM5：703）

时　　代：商代晚期
尺　　寸：通长 28、柄宽 2.5 厘米
出土地点：河南安阳殷墟妇好墓
现 藏 地：中国考古博物馆

Ruler-shaped Bronze Ware with Loong Head
Late Shang
Length 28 cm, handle width 2.5 cm
Excavated from Fuhao Tomb, Ruins of Yin, Anyang, Henan Province
Chinese Archaeological Museum

　　龙首形饰，龙头作侧视相，结构完整，头端为龙形，张嘴露齿，上颚二齿，下颚一齿，獠牙粗壮，顶部为锯齿状，圆眼，边缘凸起，"目"字形眼，独角竖立，唇下垂，短身卷尾，竖看似"冠"。在龙身的下侧有一倒夔，两者巧妙地合为一体。夔口衔扁平长条形柄，柄的下端较宽，厚钝无刃，上端饰云纹和三角形纹，线条简练清晰。

铜龙首尺形器（1976AXTM5：701）

时　　代：商代晚期
尺　　寸：通长 28.3、柄宽 2.5 厘米
出土地点：河南安阳殷墟妇好墓
现 藏 地：中国考古博物馆

Ruler-shaped Bronze Ware with Loong Head
Late Shang
Length 28.3 cm, handle width 2.5 cm
Excavated from Fuhao Tomb, Ruins of Yin, Anyang, Henan Province
Chinese Archaeological Museum

　　龙首形饰，龙头作侧视相，向右式，头端为龙形，顶部为锯齿状，顶部右端残缺，圆眼，边缘凸起，"目"字形眼，独角竖立，唇下垂，短身卷尾，竖看似"冠"。在龙身的下侧有一倒夔，两者巧妙地合为一体。夔口衔扁平长条形柄，柄的下端较宽，厚钝无刃，上端饰云纹和三角形纹，线条简练清晰。

铜龙纹盘（1977AXTM18：14）

时　　代：商代晚期
尺　　寸：通高 11.2、口径 32.7、圈足高 4.6 厘米
出土地点：河南安阳殷墟遗址
现 藏 地：中国考古博物馆

Bronze Plate with Loong Design
Late Shang
Height 11.2 cm, mouth diameter 32.7 cm, ring foot height
4.6 cm
Excavated from Ruins of Yin, Anyang, Henan Province
Chinese Archaeological Museum

平面呈圆形，敞口窄沿，腹壁较直，腹下部敛，底近平，圈足直而高，上有三个方形小孔。口沿下表面饰带状云雷纹一周，间饰目雷纹，近似一首二身的夔形。圈足饰饕餮纹三组，椭圆形目，细窄鼻梁，身分两歧，下体长尾上卷。盘内底是鱼龙纹。龙纹饰于盘底，龙头作正视相，头上两钝角，圆眼，龙体由颈部至尾盘坐两圈，体饰菱形纹，两侧填小三角纹，腹下部是圆圈纹。龙颈上部有一夔，大头，张口，身尾细长，头与龙角相对，龙纹与夔纹均匀精致。口沿下饰鱼纹一周，共 12 条，靠龙尾的 3 条稍大头，鳍尾分明，线条简练。

铜盘出现于商代早期，至晚期开始流行，为宴前饭后行沃盥之礼的盛水器。此件铜盘的纹饰布局严谨，展现出龙的神韵与力量，体现了商代青铜制造技艺的高超水平。

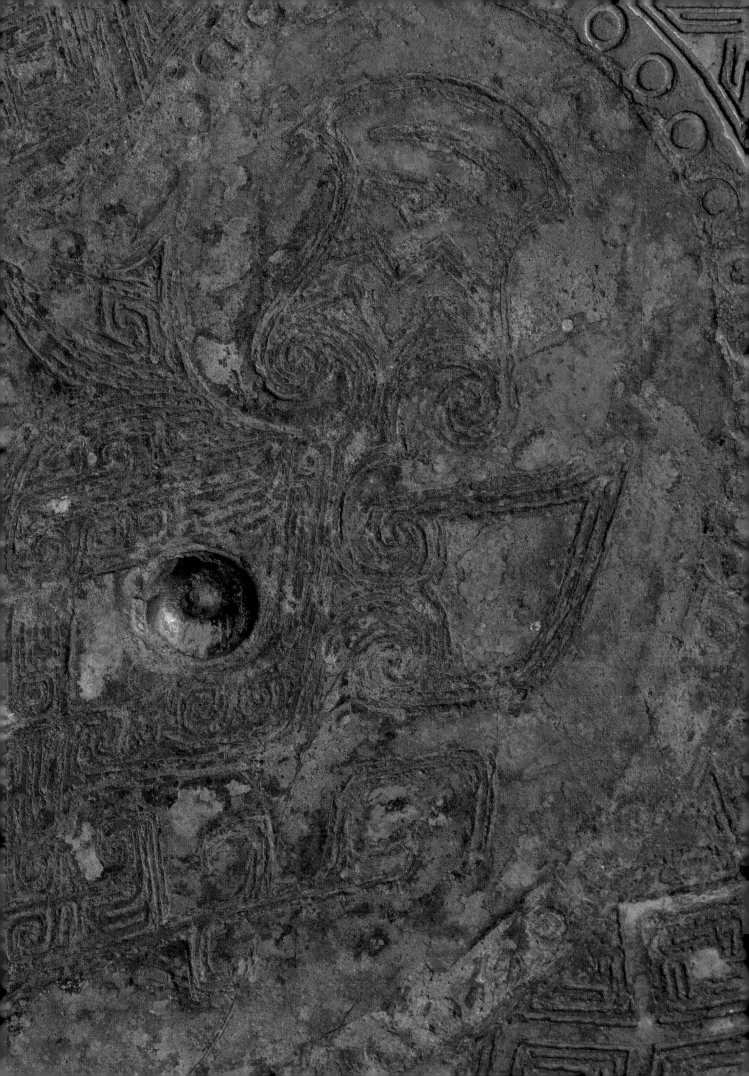

玉龙（1976AXTM5：469）

时　　代：商代晚期
尺　　寸：直径 7.8 厘米
出土地点：河南安阳殷墟妇好墓
现 藏 地：中国考古博物馆

Jade Loong
Late Shang
Diameter 7.8 cm
Excavated from Fuhao Tomb, Ruins of Yin, Anyang, Henan Province
Chinese Archaeological Museum

　　黄褐色，两面均饰龙纹，龙首、尾衔接，背脊作扁棱形，形制规整。龙口微张，露齿，角向后，"目"字形眼，尾尖外卷，身、尾饰云纹。该形制的玉龙是妇好墓出土玉龙中最多的一类。

玉龙（1976AXTM5：600）

时　　代：商代晚期
尺　　寸：直径 5.5 厘米
出土地点：河南安阳殷墟妇好墓
现 藏 地：中国考古博物馆

Jade Loong
Late Shang
Diameter 5.5 cm
Excavated from Fuhao Tomb, Ruins of Yin, Anyang, Henan Province
Chinese Archaeological Museum

淡绿色，玉质较好。两面均饰蟠龙纹，龙的首、尾衔接，背脊作扉棱形，形制规整。龙张口露齿，方形目，尾尖外卷，身、尾饰云纹。颈上有小孔，边宽孔小，孔周两面凸起呈圆口状。

玉龙（1976AXTM5：384）

时　　代：商代晚期
尺　　寸：直径 6—6.3、厚 0.5 厘米
出土地点：河南安阳殷墟妇好墓
现 藏 地：中国考古博物馆

Jade Loong
Late Shang
Diameter 6-6.3 cm, thickness 0.5 cm
Excavated from Fuhao Tomb, Ruins of Yin, Anyang, Henan Province
Chinese Archaeological Museum

　　绿色，玉质较好。头大尾短，尾齐平。口微张，露齿，尖状角。孔呈半月形，颈上有小孔。颈饰鳞纹，身、尾饰云纹。头宽尾细、尾齐平的形制在妇好墓出土玉龙中少见。

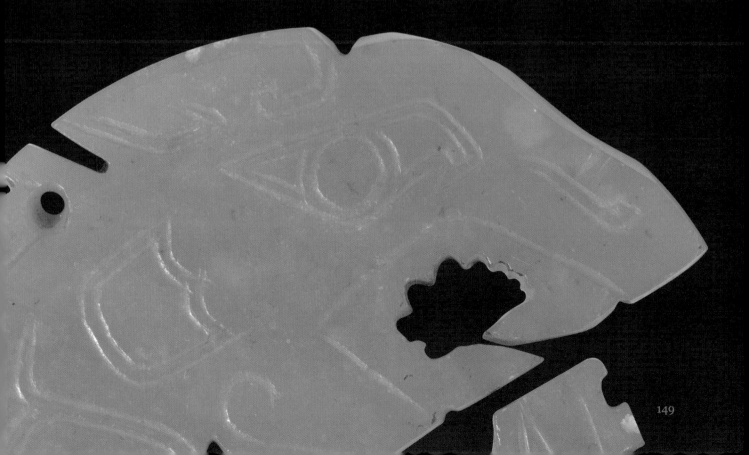

玉龙（1976AXTM5：988）

时　　代：商代晚期
尺　　寸：直径 4.8—5.1、厚 0.6 厘米
出土地点：河南安阳殷墟妇好墓
现 藏 地：中国考古博物馆

Jade Loong
Late Shang
Diameter 4.8-5.1 cm, thickness 0.6 cm
Excavated from Fuhao Tomb, Ruins of Yin, Anyang, Henan
Province
Chinese Archaeological Museum

淡黄色，有褐斑。张口露齿，角向后，身饰
云纹。颈上有孔。

玉龙（1976AXTM5∶394）

时　　代：商代晚期
尺　　寸：直径5、厚0.7厘米
出土地点：河南安阳殷墟妇好墓
现 藏 地：中国考古博物馆

Jade Loong
Late Shang
Diameter 5 cm, thickness 0.7 cm
Excavated from Fuhao Tomb, Ruins of Yin, Anyang, Henan Province
Chinese Archaeological Museum

深绿色。较厚。龙口仅钻成圆孔，未镂出牙齿。"目"字形眼，角向后，尾尖外卷。身、尾饰云纹。颈上有小孔。

玉龙（1976AXTM5：589）

时　　代：商代晚期
尺　　寸：直径9、边厚0.2厘米
出土地点：河南安阳殷墟妇好墓
现 藏 地：中国考古博物馆

Jade Loong
Late Shang
Diameter 9 cm, thickness 0.2 cm
Excavated from Fuhao Tomb, Ruins of Yin, Anyang, Henan Province
Chinese Archaeological Museum

米黄色，玉质较好，雕琢精致。边窄孔大，孔周两
面凸起呈圆口状。边雕成蟠龙形，头尾衔接，中有小缺口，
背脊刻成扁棱形，龙身有两组圆形刻线，每组由两条细
线构成。圆形刻线于缺口切割之前雕琢而成。颈部有小孔。

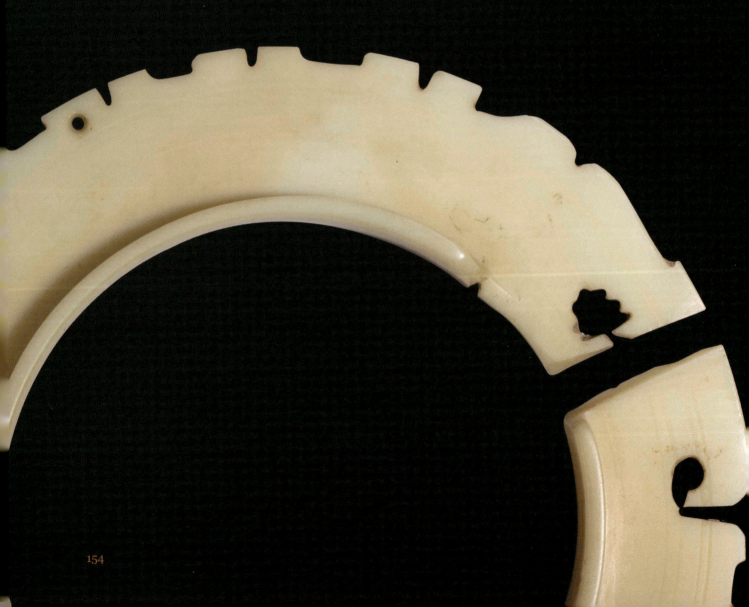

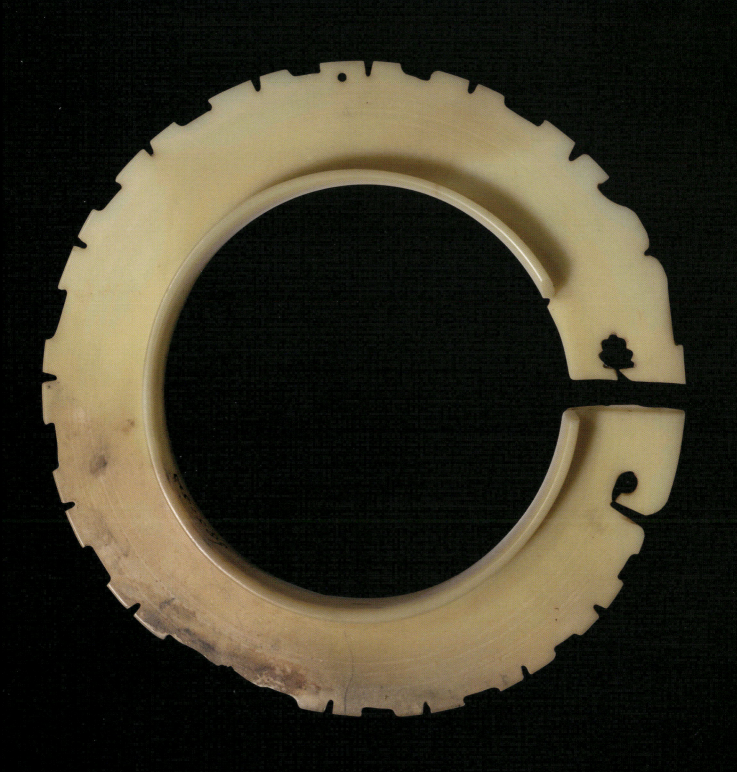

玉龙（1976AXTM5：413）

时　　代：商代晚期
尺　　寸：直径 5.8 厘米
出土地点：河南安阳殷墟妇好墓
现 藏 地：中国考古博物馆

Jade Loong
Late Shang
Diameter 5.8 cm
Excavated from Fuhao Tomb, Ruins of Yin, Anyang,
Henan Province
Chinese Archaeological Museum

　　绿色，有褐色斑沁，圆雕，体较厚。通体抛光。龙呈盘卷状，嘴微张，露舌，眼球外鼓，细眉大耳，身尾粗短。背脊雕菱形纹及三角形纹，身饰鳞纹。颈部有对钻孔。

玉龙（1976AXTM5：986）

时　　代：商代晚期
尺　　寸：直径 4.5 厘米
出土地点：河南安阳殷墟妇好墓
现 藏 地：中国考古博物馆

Jade Loong
Late Shang
Diameter 4.5 cm
Excavated from Fuhao Tomb, Ruins of Yin, Anyang, Henan
Province
Chinese Archaeological Museum

　　棕黄色，微泛绿，圆雕，体较厚。通体抛光。作盘卷状，有耳无角，身尾短粗。此龙张口露舌，圆眼，双耳上竖。背脊雕节状纹，身、尾饰云纹。孔呈椭圆形。

玉龙（1976AXTM5：414）

时　　代：商代晚期
尺　　寸：直径 4.0 厘米
出土地点：河南安阳殷墟妇好墓
现 藏 地：中国考古博物馆

Jade Loong
Late Shang
Diameter 4 cm
Excavated from Fuhao Tomb, Ruins of Yin, Anyang,
Henan Province
Chinese Archaeological Museum

　　黄褐色，圆雕，体较厚。头尾衔接，有耳无角，身尾短粗。龙体扁平，口呈一条缝，圆眼外鼓，耳上竖。背脊雕节状纹，身、尾饰云纹。颈上有小孔，其后又有一半圆形孔痕。

玉龙（1976AXTM5：435）

时　　代：商代晚期
尺　　寸：直径 4.9 厘米
出土地点：河南安阳殷墟妇好墓
现 藏 地：中国考古博物馆

Jade Loong
Late Shang
Diameter 4.9 cm
Excavated from Fuhao Tomb, Ruins of Yin, Anyang, Henan Province
Chinese Archaeological Museum

　　白色，泛黄，圆雕，体较厚。通体抛光。头尾衔接，有耳无角，身尾短粗。头、尾间缺口未完全剖开，孔不圆。一面孔周有半圆形阴线。

玉龙（1976AXTM5：424）

时　　代：商代晚期
尺　　寸：直径 5.6 厘米
出土地点：河南安阳殷墟妇好墓
现 藏 地：中国考古博物馆

Jade Loong
Late Shang
Diameter 5.6 cm
Excavated from Fuhao Tomb, Ruins of Yin, Anyang, Henan Province
Chinese Archaeological Museum

　　白色，有褐斑，浮雕。龙身作盘卷状，头尾衔接，脊背无扉棱。龙张口露齿，角向后。身、尾饰菱形纹及三角形纹，无足。

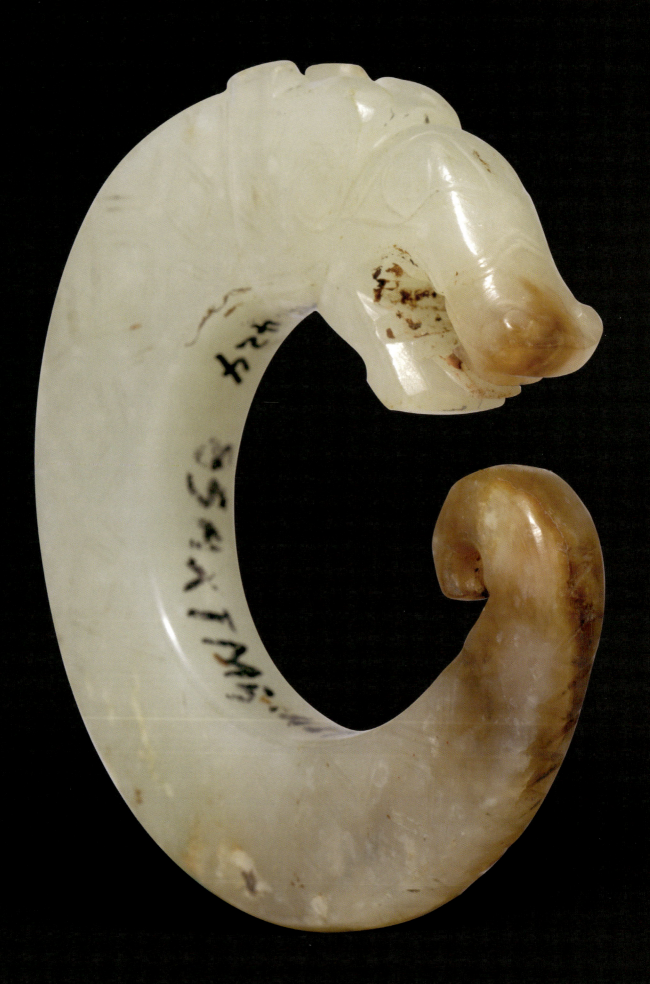

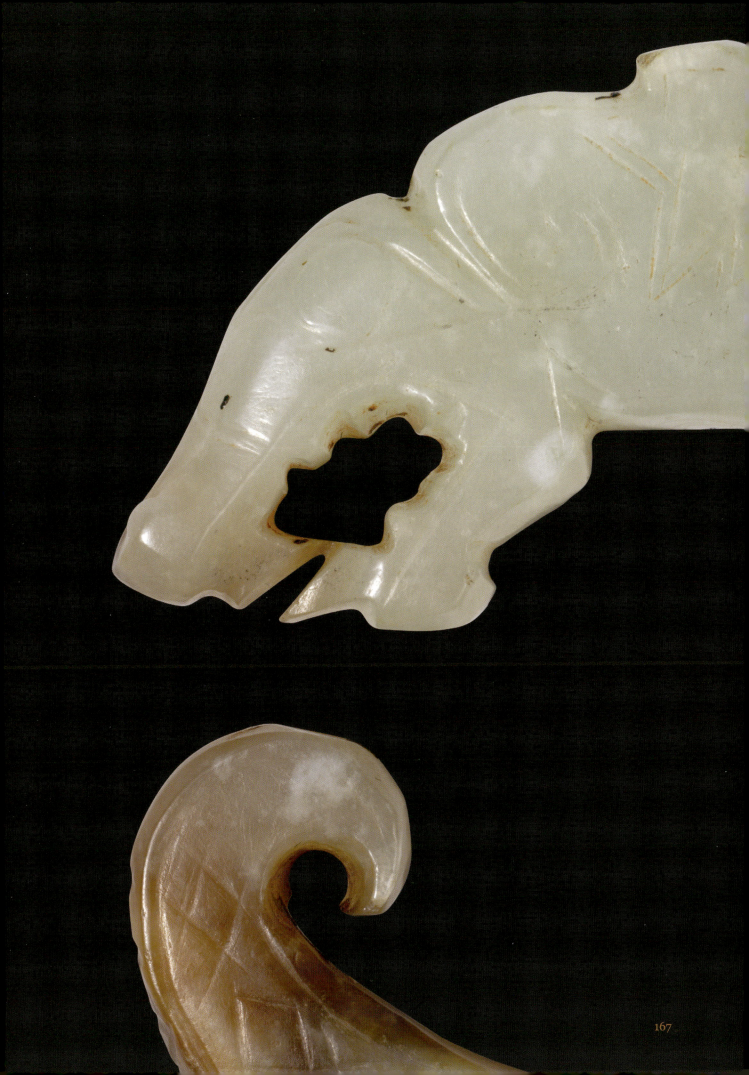

玉龙（1976AXTM5：466）

时　　代：商代晚期
尺　　寸：长径 5.2、厚 1.8 厘米
出土地点：河南安阳殷墟妇好墓
现 藏 地：中国考古博物馆

Jade Loong
Late Shang
Large diameter 5.2 cm, thickness 1.8 cm
Excavated from Fuhao Tomb, Ruins of Yin, Anyang, Henan
Province
Chinese Archaeological Museum

　　墨绿色，圆雕。通体抛光。此龙有双角和两足，头尾衔接，尾尖内卷。两角竖起，闭口，细长眉，眼珠微凸。背饰鳞纹，身两侧饰云纹，腹下刻细密短道，表示腹鳞。背上有未钻透的孔。

玉龙（1976AXTM5：422）

时　　代：商代晚期
尺　　寸：直径7、厚1.5厘米
出土地点：河南安阳殷墟妇好墓
现 藏 地：中国考古博物馆

Jade Loong
Late Shang
Diameter 7 cm, thickness 1.5 cm
Excavated from Fuhao Tomb, Ruins of Yin, Anyang, Henan
Province
Chinese Archaeological Museum

　　墨绿色。作蟠曲形，头尾衔接，中有缺口，尾尖内卷。头上有宝瓶状对角。细长眉，"目"字形眼，眼睛呈半球形。口微张，齿呈锯齿状。腹下有两短足，中脊凸起。

170

玉龙（1976AXTM5：992）

时　　代：商代晚期
尺　　寸：长9.4、高3.2厘米
出土地点：河南安阳殷墟妇好墓
现 藏 地：中国考古博物馆

Jade Loong
Late Shang
Length 9.4 cm, height 3.2 cm
Excavated from Fuhao Tomb, Ruins of Yin, Anyang, Henan Province
Chinese Archaeological Museum

淡绿色，有黄斑，圆雕。方形头，细长嘴，钝角，身尾粗短，尾尖内卷，颈下有两长方形足。身、尾饰鳞纹，腹下饰节状纹。

玉龙（1976AXTM5：995）

时　　代：商代晚期
尺　　寸：直径6、厚0.7厘米
出土地点：河南安阳殷墟妇好墓
现 藏 地：中国考古博物馆

Jade Loong
Late Shang
Diameter 6 cm, thickness 0.7 cm
Excavated from Fuhao Tomb, Ruins of Yin, Anyang, Henan
Province
Chinese Archaeological Museum

　　绿色，浮雕。龙身作盘曲状，头尾衔接，尾尖
内卷。口微张，齿细密，方形眼，角呈尖状。两面
均饰云纹，背脊抛光。

玉龙形璜（1976AXTM5：932）

时　代：商代晚期
尺　寸：残长11、宽2.6、厚0.3厘米
出土地点：河南安阳殷墟妇好墓
现藏地：中国考古博物馆

Jade *Huang* in the Shape of Loong
Late Shang
Length 11 cm, width 2.6 cm, thickness 0.3 cm
Excavated from Fuhao Tomb, Ruins of Yin, Anyang, Henan Province
Chinese Archaeological Museum

178

玉龙（1976AXTM5：995）

时　　代：商代晚期
尺　　寸：直径 6、厚 0.7 厘米
出土地点：河南安阳殷墟妇好墓
现 藏 地：中国考古博物馆

Jade Loong
Late Shang
Diameter 6 cm, thickness 0.7 cm
Excavated from Fuhao Tomb, Ruins of Yin, Anyang, Henan
Province
Chinese Archaeological Museum

　　绿色，浮雕。龙身作盘曲状，头尾衔接，尾尖
内卷。口微张，齿细密，方形眼，角呈尖状。两面
均饰云纹，背脊抛光。

玉龙形璜（1976AXTM5：1024）

时　代：商代晚期
尺　寸：直径7.5、宽1.6、厚0.4厘米
出土地点：河南安阳殷墟妇好墓
现　藏　地：中国考古博物馆

Jade *Huang* in the Shape of Loong
Late Shang
Diameter 7.5 cm, width 1.6 cm, thickness 0.4 cm
Excavated from Fuhao Tomb, Ruins of Yin, Anyang, Henan
Province
Chinese Archaeological Museum

青白色，可见絮状物。微透光。器身局部有土色及褐色沁。弧度大于半圆。龙口呈圆形，未雕齿，上唇微翘。两面抛光，无纹饰，似半成品。

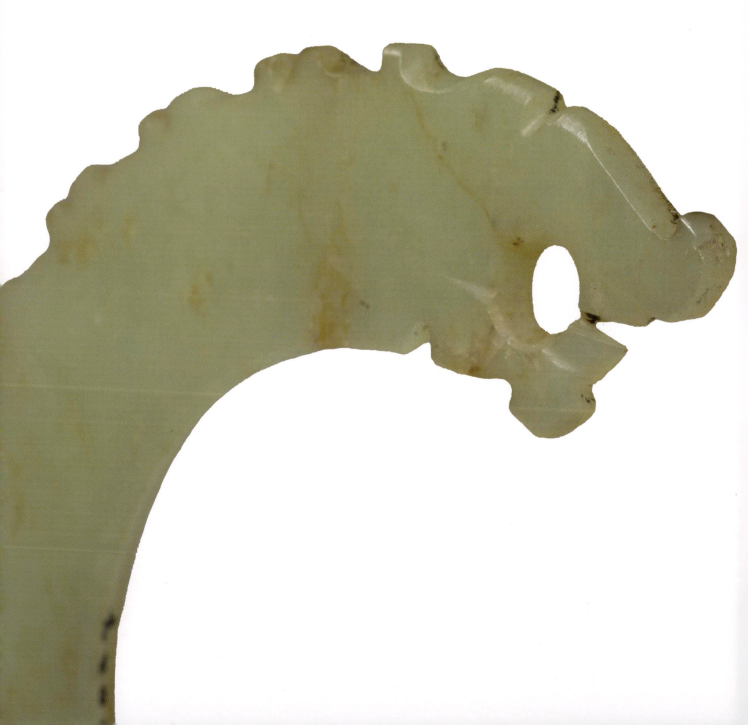

玉龙形璜（1976AXTM5：932）

时　　代：商代晚期
尺　　寸：残长 11、宽 2.6、厚 0.3 厘米
出土地点：河南安阳殷墟妇好墓
现 藏 地：中国考古博物馆

Jade *Huang* in the Shape of Loong
Late Shang
Length 11 cm, width 2.6 cm, thickness 0.3 cm
Excavated from Fuhao Tomb, Ruins of Yin, Anyang, Henan Province
Chinese Archaeological Museum

青白色玉，可见絮状物及节理面，微透光。油脂光泽明显，局部有糖色沁。张口露齿，上唇翘，"目"字形眼，一角向后，颈饰鳞纹，身、尾饰变形云纹。背脊与腹均雕成扁棱形。尾端稍残，尾尖上卷。

玉龙形璜（1976AXTM5：391）

时　　代：商代晚期
尺　　寸：直径 7.8、宽 1.7、厚 0.2 厘米
出土地点：河南安阳殷墟妇好墓
现 藏 地：中国考古博物馆

Jade *Huang* in the Shape of Loong
Late Shang
Diameter 7.8 cm, width 1.7 cm, thickness 0.2 cm
Excavated from Fuhao Tomb, Ruins of Yin, Anyang, Henan
Province
Chinese Archaeological Museum

白色，有黄斑。弧度大于半圆。龙上、下门齿相连，方形目，一角向后，足前屈，雕四爪，尾尖上卷，脊背雕作扉棱形。颈饰鳞纹，身、尾饰变形云纹。

玉夔首刻刀（1976AXTM5：936）

时　　代：商代晚期
尺　　寸：长6、宽2.7、刃宽0.7、厚0.2厘米
出土地点：河南安阳殷墟妇好墓
现 藏 地：中国考古博物馆

Jade Engraving Knife in the Shape of *Kui*-loong
Late Shang
Length 6 cm, width 2.7 cm, blade width 0.7 cm,
thickness 0.2 cm
Excavated from Fuhao Tomb, Ruins of Yin, Anyang,
Henan Province
Chinese Archaeological Museum

大头张口，身分两歧，长尾，尾末刻出斜刃，
刃由两面磨成，口后有小孔。身上刻纹不甚清晰。

玉龙（2001HDM54：450）

时　　代：商代晚期
尺　　寸：直径 5.67、厚 0.92 厘米
出土地点：河南安阳殷墟遗址
现 藏 地：殷墟博物馆

Jade Loong
Late Shang
Diameter 5.67 cm, thickness 0.92 cm
Excavated from Ruins of Yin, Anyang, Henan Province
Yinxu Museum

　　青绿色，吻部前凸。脊背上雕刻扉棱，以七组同型图案构成。首与尾之间未分开，中部半圆弧形穿孔。器身两面饰以卷云纹。

玉龙（1977AGGM701：87）

时　　代：商代晚期
尺　　寸：高 3.53、宽 2.39、厚 1.49 厘米
出土地点：河南安阳殷墟遗址
现 藏 地：殷墟博物馆

Jade Loong
Late Shang
Height 3.53 cm, width 2.39 cm, thickness 1.49 cm
Excavated from Ruins of Yin, Anyang, Henan Province
Yinxu Museum

　　青色，匀净。首、尾相连。吻部翘起。面部内凹。双眼凸出。双耳竖立外撇。以阴线表现前足与卷尾。中部有对钻孔。该玉龙头部似猪，体似虫形，这也体现出中国古代文明中龙的形象是综合了多种动物的特征演化而来。

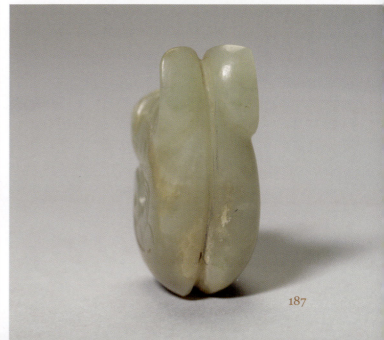

玉龙形觿（2001HDM54：370）

时　　代：商代晚期
尺　　寸：通长 8.83、尾长 4.69、厚 0.55 厘米
出土地点：河南安阳殷墟遗址
现 藏 地：殷墟博物馆

Jade *Xi* in the Shape of Loong
Late Shang
Length 8.83 cm, tail length 4.69 cm, thickness 0.55 cm
Excavated from Ruins of Yin, Anyang, Henan Province
Yinxu Museum

青色，尾部有褐斑，通体光素无纹。夔龙回首，下颌与背部连接，面部下凹，吻部前凸，双犄角凸起，前后腿作蹲踞状，龙尾上翘。玉觿出现于商代晚期，可能与以实用为目的的角（骨）觿，或者是与佩戴兽牙的传统相关。

玉龙（1977AGGM701：1）

时　　代：商代晚期
尺　　寸：通长 5.17、厚 0.35 厘米
出土地点：河南安阳殷墟遗址
现 藏 地：殷墟博物馆

Jade Loong
Late Shang
Length 5.17 cm, thickness 0.35 cm
Excavated from Ruins of Yin, Anyang, Henan Province
Yinxu Museum

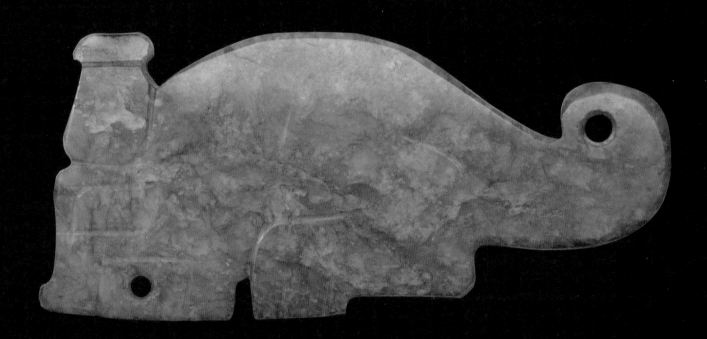

灰褐色。龙首下垂，口部双面钻孔，方目，宝瓶状独角，弓背，足前屈，尾部上卷。

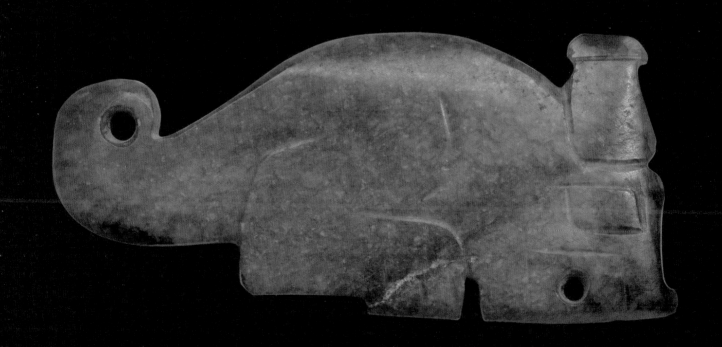

玉龙（1996 钢东路 M79：4-1）

时　　代：商代晚期
尺　　寸：长 9、宽 3 厘米
出土地点：河南安阳殷墟遗址
现 藏 地：中国考古博物馆

Jade Loong
Late Shang
Length 9 cm, width 3 cm
Excavated from Ruins of Yin, Anyang, Henan Province
Chinese Archaeological Museum

片状两面雕玉龙，龙首与身躯都呈侧视的平面形象。头顶立角，凸鼻，头低平向下，吻部穿一孔。

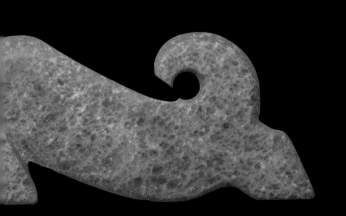

玉龙（1996 钢东路 M79：4-2）

时　　代：商代晚期
尺　　寸：长 8.8、宽 2.9 厘米
出土地点：河南安阳殷墟遗址
现 藏 地：中国考古博物馆

Jade Loong
Late Shang
Length 8.8 cm, width 2.9 cm
Excavated from Ruins of Yin, Anyang, Henan Province
Chinese Archaeological Museum

片状两面雕玉龙，龙首与身躯都呈侧视的平面形象。头顶立角，凸鼻，头低平向下，吻部穿一孔。

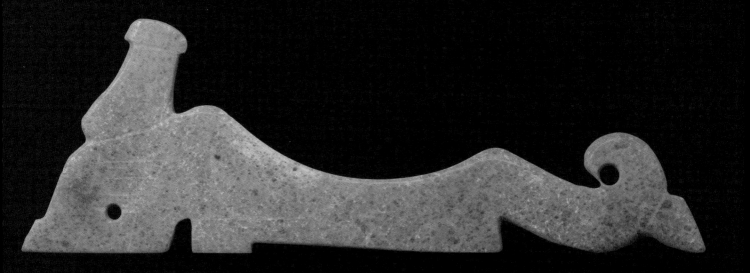

玉龙（1976AWBM4：2）

时　　代：商代晚期
尺　　寸：长3.1、宽2.7厘米
出土地点：河南安阳殷墟遗址
现 藏 地：中国考古博物馆

Jade Loong
Late Shang
Length 3.1 cm, width 2.7 cm
Excavated from Ruins of Yin, Anyang, Henan Province
Chinese Archaeological Museum

　　龙身卷曲，首尾相连，头部有两个圆孔。

玉龙（1989ASNM90：80）

时　　代：商代晚期
尺　　寸：长 5.5、宽 3 厘米
出土地点：河南安阳殷墟遗址
现 藏 地：中国考古博物馆

Jade Loong
Late Shang
Length 5.5 cm, width 3 cm
Excavated from Ruins of Yin, Anyang, Henan Province
Chinese Archaeological Museum

　　整体呈首尾相对的勾卷状。吻部略前凸，头上有角孔。

玉龙（2004ASPM9：10）

时　　代：商代晚期
尺　　寸：长 3.3、宽 3.2 厘米
出土地点：河南安阳殷墟遗址
现 藏 地：中国考古博物馆

Jade Loong
Late Shang
Length 3.3 cm, width 3.2 cm
Excavated from Ruins of Yin, Anyang, Henan Province
Chinese Archaeological Museum

虺首玉龙，整体呈首尾相对的勾卷状。吻部呈扁状前凸，器身阴线雕刻勾角卷云纹。

绿松石夔龙（1972ASM373：12）

时　　代：商代晚期
尺　　寸：长 4.3、宽 2.6 厘米
出土地点：河南安阳殷墟遗址
现 藏 地：殷墟博物馆

Turquoise *Kui*-loong
Late Shang
Length 4.3 cm, width 2.6 cm
Excavated from Ruins of Yin, Anyang, Henan Province
Yinxu Museum

　　正面绿色，另一面黄灰色。龙首回顾。张口，上唇外卷。方眼。卷角。角上有穿孔。身躯向上扬起。尾略残。

石龙钮形器盖（1976AXTM5：49）

时　　代：商代晚期
尺　　寸：高 3、长径 5.4、短径 4.5 厘米
出土地点：河南安阳殷墟妇好墓
现 藏 地：中国考古博物馆

Stone Lid with Loong-shaped Knob
Late Shang
Height 3 cm, large diameter 5.4 cm,
small diameter 4.5 cm
Excavated from Fuhao Tomb, Ruins of Yin, Anyang,
Henan Province
Chinese Archaeological Museum

　　白色，微灰，大理岩。椭圆形，面部微鼓，上雕龙形钮，龙口微张，露舌，眼、耳、鼻清晰，双足前屈，作伏状，尾盘于边沿，背、尾均饰菱形纹；背面略凹，中间刻"十"字形阴线，长径上、下侧各雕夔龙纹一对，头相对，张口，身、尾极短。也有观点认为此物是印章，印纹上的形象是三龙一凤，龙、凤皆是殷墟时期重要的幻想动物纹饰主题。

石龙纹磬

时　　代：商代晚期
尺　　寸：长 87、高 28.5、厚 4.5 厘米
出土地点：河南安阳殷墟遗址
现 藏 地：中国考古博物馆

Chime Stone with Loong Design
Late Shang
Length 87 cm, height 28.5 cm, thickness 4.5 cm
Excavated from Ruins of Yin, Anyang, Henan Province
Chinese Archaeological Museum

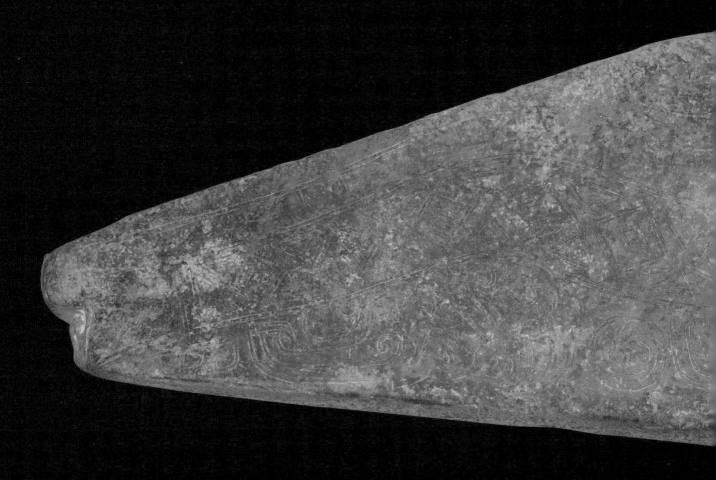

206

石磬两面均以双勾线条雕刻出大型长躯夔龙纹，线条遒劲，匀称地布满整个磬面，与器身浑然一体。龙口张开，两眼圆睁，四爪锐利。悬孔有磨损痕迹，显然是一件久经使用的古乐器。与1950年殷墟武官村大墓出土的虎纹石磬并称"商磬双璧"。

骨夔首笄（1976AXTM5：180）

时　　代：商代晚期
尺　　寸：残长 17.5 厘米
出土地点：河南安阳殷墟妇好墓
现 藏 地：中国考古博物馆

Bone Hairpin with *Kui*-loong Design
Late Shang
Length 17.5 cm
Excavated from Fuhao Tomb, Ruins of Yin, Anyang, Henan
Province
Chinese Archaeological Museum

　　夔龙形首，稍残。夔龙作倒立状，张口露齿，"目"字形眼，身、尾周缘刻出锯齿形薄棱，棱上钻有排列匀称的小圆孔，笄杆从夔龙口出，最大径在上端，往下渐收缩成尖状。精巧光洁。

211

骨夔首笄（1976AXTM5：177）

时　　代：商代晚期
尺　　寸：长 20.6 厘米
出土地点：河南安阳殷墟妇好墓
现 藏 地：中国考古博物馆

Bone Hairpin with *Kui*-loong Design
Late Shang
Length 20.6 cm
Excavated from Fuhao Tomb, Ruins of Yin, Anyang, Henan Province
Chinese Archaeological Museum

骨夔首笄（1976AXTM5：179）

时　　代：商代晚期
尺　　寸：残长 20.9 厘米
出土地点：河南安阳殷墟妇好墓
现 藏 地：中国考古博物馆

Bone Hairpin with *Kui*-loong Design
Late Shang
Length 20.9 cm
Excavated from Fuhao Tomb, Ruins of Yin, Anyang, Henan Province
Chinese Archaeological Museum

刻辞卜骨（屯南 942/H24：171）

时　　代：商代晚期
出土地点：河南安阳殷墟小屯南地
现 藏 地：中国考古博物馆

Inscribed Oracle Bone
Late Shang
Excavated from southern area of Xiaotun, Ruins of Yin, Anyang,
Henan Province
Chinese Archaeological Museum

　　右下角卜辞释作"易龙兵"，"易"即"赐"，
为赏赐之意；"龙"可能为人名或兵器名；"兵"
可能指武器或兵士，皆难以明断。但本辞显然与军
事相关，或是战前颁赐，或是战胜后行赏赐。

942（H24：171）　　　摹本號：58　　骨　　　康丁

背面有鑿、灼，鑿屬四型一式。骨沿A式。

(1) 弜☑龍☑？吉。

(2) 昜龍兵？

(3) 戍尋？

(4) 王叀因弓令从☑？

(5) 弜？吉。

龍：也可能是龔。

昜：當爲賜。

戍尋：戍爲官名，尋爲人名。

（資料來源：《小屯南地甲骨》）

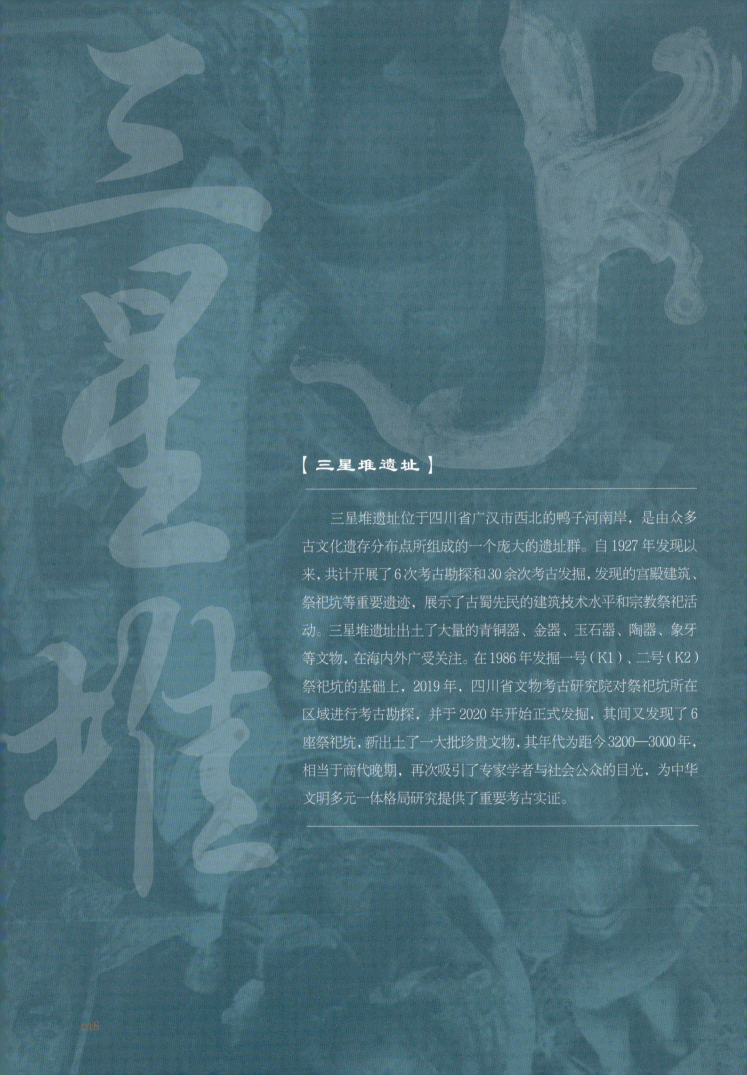

【 三星堆遗址 】

三星堆遗址位于四川省广汉市西北的鸭子河南岸，是由众多古文化遗存分布点所组成的一个庞大的遗址群。自1927年发现以来，共计开展了6次考古勘探和30余次考古发掘，发现的宫殿建筑、祭祀坑等重要遗迹，展示了古蜀先民的建筑技术水平和宗教祭祀活动。三星堆遗址出土了大量的青铜器、金器、玉石器、陶器、象牙等文物，在海内外广受关注。在1986年发掘一号（K1）、二号（K2）祭祀坑的基础上，2019年，四川省文物考古研究院对祭祀坑所在区域进行考古勘探，并于2020年开始正式发掘，其间又发现了6座祭祀坑，新出土了一大批珍贵文物，其年代为距今3200—3000年，相当于商代晚期，再次吸引了专家学者与社会公众的目光，为中华文明多元一体格局研究提供了重要考古实证。

四川广汉三星堆遗址铜猪鼻龙形器出土情况
（四川省文物考古研究院供图）

铜猪鼻龙形器（K8 ⑨：400）

时　　代：商
尺　　寸：长 119、通高 40 厘米
出土地点：四川广汉三星堆遗址
现 藏 地：四川省文物考古研究院

Loong-shaped Bronze Ware
Shang Dynasty
Length 119 cm, height 40 cm
Excavated from Sanxingdui site, Guanghan, Sichuan Province
Sichuan Archeology Research Institute

　　出土于八号祭祀坑，此前三星堆遗址从未发现该类器物。体形硕大，圆柱形。吻部前端较扁平，前凸，周围饰一圈带孔牙璋图案及阴刻弦纹。鼻子呈中空的长方形，双眼凸出，尖耳向前弯曲，头部与身体间隔以环形宽带纹，两侧各有一圆角三棱形纹饰。身体两侧饰以刀形羽纹，腹下饰波浪纹。尾部末端有 3 个圆形穿孔。圆筒状腰身，造型奇特，是三星堆先民在吸收华夏文明龙形象基础之上的创新创造。

铜龙首形饰（K3QW：281）

时　　代：商
尺　　寸：高 23、宽 15、厚 1.5 厘米
出土地点：四川广汉三星堆遗址
现 藏 地：四川省文物考古研究院

Bronze Ornament in the Shape of Loong Head
Shang Dynasty
Height 23 cm, width 15 cm, thickness 1.5 cm
Excavated from Sanxingdui site, Guanghan, Sichuan Province
Sichuan Archeology Research Institute

　　器物整体扁平，龙首张口，獠牙大而尖利，鼻部呈卷云状，头顶有一向后弯曲的犄角，耳部后弯，耳尖下折，颈部以下为方形插销，中有方形开孔。此器物出土时与多件器物粘连。

铜顶璋龙头（K7QW-T-419）

时　　代：商
尺　　寸：长 4.8、宽 2.4、高 9.1 厘米
出土地点：四川广汉三星堆遗址
现 藏 地：四川省文物考古研究院

Bronze Ornament in the Shape of Loong Headed *Zhang*
Shang Dynasty
Length 4.8 cm, width 2.4 cm, height 9.1 cm
Excavated from Sanxingdui site, Guanghan, Sichuan Province
Sichuan Archeology Research Institute

张口露齿，下吻内卷，"臣"字形眼，龙角仅存一只，细长微卷，龙耳向后勾卷，前腿和龙爪均为浅浮雕。龙头上顶牙璋，璋两面扁平，前端分叉，两侧各饰三齿。龙身中空，呈銎状，推测为铜器附件。

铜尖耳龙形器（K7QW-T-312）

时　　代：商
尺　　寸：长 13.4、宽 2、高 13.2 厘米
出土地点：四川广汉三星堆遗址
现 藏 地：四川省文物考古研究院

Loong-shaped Bronze Ware
Shang Dynasty
Length 13.4 cm, width 2 cm, height 13.2 cm
Excavated from Sanxingdui site, Guanghan, Sichuan Province
Sichuan Archeology Research Institute

　　尖牙巨口，上吻上卷，下吻较短，微内卷，长舌下垂，舌尖连接圆环，或为连接挂饰之用。尖状竖耳，长颈弯曲，末段有羽翅状凸起，身躯残断，其功能尚未可知。

【前掌大墓地】

前掌大墓地位于山东省滕州市官桥镇前掌大村，薛河下游西岸。前四次发掘主要集中在北区墓地，发掘面积约3000平方米，揭露出龙山文化遗存、商代中期居住遗迹、商代晚期灰沟及商代晚期墓葬，清理各类墓葬30座。南区墓地发掘面积亦约3000平方米，清理出商末周初的居住址、壕沟、夯土台、灰坑水井、祭祀设施、车马坑、殉牛马坑及70余座墓葬。对于研究商周时期东方方国的政治、经济、文化、族属等问题具有重大意义。

玉鸟（M120∶64）

时　　代：商末周初
尺　　寸：长 9.2、宽 2.1 厘米
出土地点：山东滕州前掌大墓地
现 藏 地：中国考古博物馆

Jade Bird
Late Shang and Early Zhou Dynasties
Length 9.2 cm, width 2.1 cm
Excavated from Qianzhangdai Cemetery, Tengzhou, Shandong Province
Chinese Archaeological Museum

　　淡绿色，发黄或有黄、黑色沁痕，微透明，通体光滑。作站立状，头微抬，圆眼，吻部前伸，身体饰单阴线刻划纹饰。

玉鸟（M38：11）

时　　代：商末周初
尺　　寸：长 6.54、厚 0.3 厘米
出土地点：山东滕州前掌大墓地
现 藏 地：中国考古博物馆

Jade Bird
Late Shang and Early Zhou Dynasties
Length 6.54 cm, thickness 0.3 cm
Excavated from Qianzhangdai Cemetery, Tengzhou, Shandong Province
Chinese Archaeological Museum

　　淡绿色，发黄或有黄、黑色沁痕，微透明，通体光滑。作站立状，头微抬，圆眼，钩喙，身体饰单阴线刻划纹饰。

玉龙形璜（M11：68）

时　　代：商末周初
尺　　寸：长 10.8、宽 3 厘米
出土地点：山东滕州前掌大墓地
现 藏 地：中国考古博物馆

Loong-shaped Jade Huang
Late Shang and Early Zhou Dynasties
Length 10.8 cm, width 3 cm
Excavated from Qianzhangdai Cemetery, Tengzhou, Shandong Province
Chinese Archaeological Museum

　　淡青色，半透明，通体光滑。整体造型似为一条龙，身体镂空，以减地法刻划出眼睛及其他纹饰，纹饰由 4 条较小的龙盘旋构成。

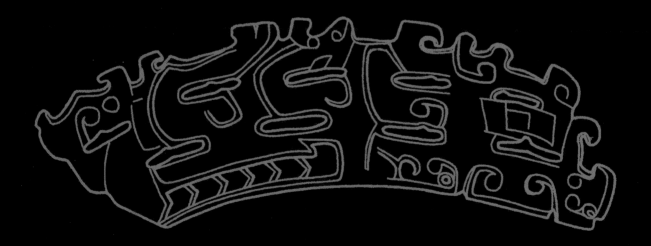

玉龙形璜（M120：56）

时　　代：商末周初
尺　　寸：长11.7、宽3.4厘米
出土地点：山东滕州前掌大墓地
现 藏 地：中国考古博物馆

Loong-shaped Jade *Huang*
Late Shang and Early Zhou Dynasties
Length 11.7 cm, width 3.4 cm
Excavated from Qianzhangdai Cemetery, Tengzhou, Shandong Province
Chinese Archaeological Museum

　　暗绿色，带深绿色沁点，不透明，弧长近整圆的二分之一。两面双阴线刻划出头、睛、口、耳、角、爪等部位，大方口内对钻一圆孔，"臣"字形目、圆睛、桃叶状耳、角后倾，边缘经打磨。

233

玉龙形觿（M132：9）

时　　代：商末周初
尺　　寸：长9.2、宽1.5厘米
出土地点：山东滕州前掌大墓地
现 藏 地：中国考古博物馆

Loong-shaped Jade *Xi*
Late Shang and Early Zhou Dynasties
Length 9.2 cm, width 1.5 cm
Excavated from Qianzhangdai Cemetery, Tengzhou, Shandong Province
Chinese Archaeological Museum

　　乳白色，半透明，圆润光滑。整体为一龙的造型。龙头较为夸张，大张口，舌前伸形成尖部，龙尾卷曲于头后。双面雕，以减地法刻划出头、睛、耳及身。刃部以减地法刻划出简化的蝉纹。柄部末端对钻一圆孔。

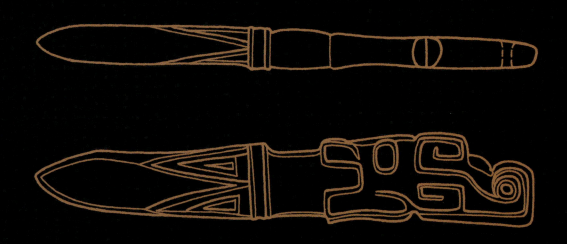

玉龙（M119：18）

时　　代：商末周初
尺　　寸：长 3.1、宽 2.8、厚 0.4 厘米
出土地点：山东滕州前掌大墓地
现 藏 地：中国考古博物馆

Jade Loong
Late Shang and Early Zhou Dynasties
Length 3.1 cm, width 2.8 cm, thickness 0.4 cm
Excavated from Qianzhangdai Cemetery, Tengzhou, Shandong
Province
Chinese Archaeological Museum

　　黄白色，有褐色斑点。龙身蟠曲，首尾相衔，中有缺口。张口，卷鼻大眼，头顶有瓶状角，龙身上刻有鱼鳞纹。两面花纹相同。背上和尾部各有一穿孔。

237

玉龙（M119：19）

时　　代：商末周初
尺　　寸：长 3.1、宽 2.9、厚 0.4 厘米
出土地点：山东滕州前掌大墓地
现 藏 地：中国考古博物馆

Jade Loong
Late Shang and Early Zhou Dynasties
Length 3.1 cm, width 2.9 cm, thickness 0.4 cm
Excavated from Qianzhangdai Cemetery, Tengzhou, Shandong
Province
Chinese Archaeological Museum

黄白色，有褐色斑点。龙身蟠曲，首尾相衔，中有缺口。张口，卷鼻大眼，头顶有瓶状角，龙身上刻有鱼鳞纹。两面花纹相同。背上和尾部各有一穿孔。

【 西周 】

　　西周早期的龙，基本延续了商代龙的形象，有的龙身如旋涡盘卷，新出现了人龙合体的艺术造型。经过西周中期的礼仪变革，至西周中晚期，龙的形象为硕头长角，长吻上卷，装饰敦厚华美，人龙合体的造型更加丰富，尽显周代崇龙礼仪及人龙合一思想观念的发展成熟。

铜钺（M199：10）

时　　代：西周
尺　　寸：长14.8、宽8.7厘米
出土地点：陕西长安张家坡西周墓地
现 藏 地：中国考古博物馆

Bronze *Yue*
Western Zhou Dynasty
Length 14.8 cm, width 8.7 cm
Excavated from Zhangjiapo Cemetery, Chang'an,
Shaanxi Province
Chinese Archaeological Museum

　　器身较扁，上窄下宽，刃宽阔，弧状，刃角上翘。器身中部有一较大圆孔。两穿，穿孔近阑，位于器身外侧。直阑，阑之两端出于钺身以外。直内，内部为长方形，中部有一较小之圆孔。钺身中部圆孔周边盘卷着一条浅浮雕式游龙，龙身伸向阑部，龙头搭在阑部正中，作浮雕样昂起，龙嘴已经伸到内部，两面的龙头成为阑后的两个小翼。钺身两侧各附着有一条夔龙。夔首反顾，夔身作波浪形起伏，翘尾。夔首近阑，夔角与阑之间的空档即为钺穿。夔尾末端与刃角相接而同时上翘。钺身近阑处之龙颈两旁各有一个圆涡纹，钺身前部饰曲折纹和简化蝉纹。龙身饰短线纹以象征龙体之花纹，夔身用鳞纹来表示有鳞甲。内后端饰曲尺状阴线纹。刃部有较多小缺口，似为实用品。钺作为中国古代政治权力的重要象征，位列"九命之锡"，是王权统治的重要表现形式。

玉龙（M121：29）

时　　代：西周
尺　　寸：长4.4、宽3.7、厚0.4厘米
出土地点：陕西长安张家坡西周墓地
现 藏 地：中国考古博物馆

Jade Loong
Western Zhou Dynasty
Length 4.4 cm, width 3.7 cm, thickness 0.4 cm
Excavated from Zhangjiapo Cemetery, Chang'an, Shaanxi Province
Chinese Archaeological Museum

透闪石软玉，黄绿色。卷鼻大眼，张口露齿，头顶有瓶状角，屈体卷尾，腹下一足双爪，龙身上刻卷云纹，两面花纹相同。鼻上有一小穿孔。

玉柄形饰（M121∶30）

时　代：西周
尺　寸：长9.7、宽3.5、厚0.3厘米
出土地点：陕西长安张家坡西周墓地
现藏地：中国考古博物馆

Handle-shaped Ornament
Western Zhou Dynasty
Length 9.7 cm, width 3.5 cm, thickness 0.3 cm
Excavated from Zhangjiapo Cemetery, Chang'an, Shaanxi Province
Chinese Archaeological Museum

　　透闪石软玉，灰绿色有褐斑。器形为长方形牌状，上宽下窄，顶端有一组扉牙，两侧各有两组扉牙，末端圆弧，似是榫。器身两面刻相同的一鸟一龙纹。鸟纹在上，钩喙，圆睛，头有花冠，扬翅，卷尾，胸下有硕大的鸟爪。龙纹在下，卷鼻，张口，"臣"字形目，顾首，龙身曲折，尾下垂，胸下有爪。

玉龙凤人物形佩饰（M157：104）

时　　代：西周
尺　　寸：长 6.8、宽 2.4、厚 0.5 厘米
出土地点：陕西长安张家坡西周墓地
现 藏 地：中国考古博物馆

Jade Pendant with Loong, Phoenix and Human Design
Western Zhou Dynasty
Length 6.8 cm, width 2.4 cm, thickness 0.5 cm
Excavated from Zhangjiapo Cemetery, Chang'an, Shaanxi
Province
Chinese Archaeological Museum

青绿色，透闪石软玉。这是一件龙、凤和人物头像玉雕，分上、中、下三层。下层是一龙一凤，龙头朝上，卷鼻，方睛，有角，曲体，尾部上卷；凤则倒依于龙身之下，尖喙向上，圆睛，扬翅，尾下垂。龙和凤的身上都有双钩刻纹。中部是一条横向的屈体卷尾龙，头向下，鼻上卷，圆睛，有角，曲体，尾向内卷，龙身上也有双钩刻纹。上层一侧是一个较大的人物头像，另一侧为一个龙头，其上有一个较小的人物头像，两个人物头像均为圆雕。有两个穿孔，一个在大头像的发际，孔由一面穿透；另一个在下层的龙尾上，孔由侧面穿透。玉雕中两个人物头像似为此件玉雕的主体，三龙一凤则是人物升天的助手，体现了人龙合一的理念。这件玉雕玉质晶莹温润，花纹图案两面相同，制作精细，构思奇巧，是西周玉器中少见的艺术珍品。

东周

【 东周 】

　　东周时期，走兽之龙生出双翼，龙角夸张繁复。从玉器看，龙头变小，龙身扭动拉长，四足和尾部渐渐明晰，身体布满象征飞翔和鳞片的云纹与谷纹。龙还受到北方农牧交错地带人群的喜爱，并通过草原地带传播到欧亚大陆的中部和西部。

双龙纹瓦当（2017SYYT49⑥：1）

时　　代：战国中期
尺　　寸：直径13.4、厚1厘米
出土地点：陕西西安栎阳城遗址
现藏地：中国考古博物馆

Tile-end with Loong Design
Mid Warring States Period
Diameter 13.4 cm, thickness 1 cm
Excavated from Yueyang City site, Xi'an, Shaanxi Province
Chinese Archaeological Museum

　　二龙交织，身形细长弯曲，两眼和爪明显，刻工利落。

陶龙纹器盖（Ⅱ：7）

时　　代：战国晚期
尺　　寸：直径12.1、厚1、高2.6厘米
出土地点：陕西西安栎阳城遗址
现 藏 地：中国考古博物馆

Pottery Lid with Loong Design
Late Warring States Period
Diameter 12.1 cm, thickness 1 cm, height 2.6 cm
Excavated from Yueyang City site, Xi'an, Shaanxi Province
Chinese Archaeological Museum

面饰蟠龙，长须，二足，边沿饰横"S"纹。

人执龙形玉佩 (M1∶36)

时　　代：战国
尺　　寸：长 7.05、宽 3.95、厚 0.4 厘米
出土地点：湖北荆州院墙湾一号楚墓
现 藏 地：荆州博物馆

Jade Pendant with Human Reining Loong Design
Warring States Period
Length 7.05 cm, width 3.95 cm, thickness 0.4 cm
Excavated from Yuanqiangwan Tomb No. 1, Jingzhou,
Hubei Province
Jingzhou Museum

黄白色，有褐色沁斑。两侧为相向而立的双龙，龙背上各站立一鸟，中间为一神人，头顶一绹索纹圆环，双臂张开向下，双手各操一龙。龙上下颌饰绹索纹，身有人字形骨节纹，尾站立小鸟等特征都流行于楚式玉龙佩。神人身着紧袖长袍，袍上饰二方连续间隔长方形网纹，为东周时期中山国北狄族服饰。因此这件玉佩有可能是由楚国玉工制作，但受到中山国玉文化的影响。

鹰顶金冠饰

时　　代：战国晚期
出土地点：内蒙古杭锦旗阿鲁柴登墓葬
现 藏 地：内蒙古博物院

Gold Crown Ornament with an Eagle-shaped Top
Late Warring States Period
Excavated from Aluchaideng Tomb, Hanggin Banner, Inner
Mongolia Autonomous Region
Inner Mongolia Museum

　　鹰顶金冠饰有"草原瑰宝"之誉，是游牧部落首领的饰物，由冠顶和冠带组成。冠顶为半球形，饰浅浮雕四狼吃羊图案，中央站立一只展翅雄鹰，鹰首、颈用绿松石制成，尾部用金丝与鹰体连接。冠带由三条半圆形绳索式金带巧妙并合而成，末端分别装饰有卧羊、卧马和草原风格的龙。龙头似狼也似虎，唇鼻上翻，长角（或者是长耳）冲前，头后鬃毛飘动。

　　鹰顶金冠饰构思奇特、制作精湛、纹饰精美，是一件极具北方游牧民族文化特征的代表作。

四象形成有其历史进程，可追溯到史前，商代有一些线索。河南三门峡上村岭虢国墓地出土一枚西周晚期的四象铜镜。湖北随州战国初年墓葬出土的漆箱盖上，绘制有与二十八宿相对应的苍龙和白虎图像，证实了汉代典型四象的初步定型，即"苍龙连蜷于左，白虎猛踞于右，朱雀奋翼于前，灵龟圈首于后"。

湖北随州曾侯乙墓衣箱上的星象图
（资料来源：《曾侯乙墓》）

湖北随州曾侯乙墓衣箱上的星象图
（资料来源：《曾侯乙墓》）

261

龙泽四海

秦汉时代，中央集权的郡县制促成了大一统王朝的成熟。龙作为中华文化的核心基因，其形象和内涵也随之演变，经唐宋渐渐成为天子的象征；至元明清，皇权与龙的融合达到巅峰，龙的多维文化渐趋丰满。汉代时四象明确，宋代时龙形定样，元代时龙爪分级，明代时龙生九子，清代时黄龙为旗，龙最终成为中华文明的代表性符号，中国龙的形象和精神更加广泛地在世界传播，得到越来越多人的喜爱。

【秦汉】

秦汉时期，龙脸变长、身变细，弯弯曲曲，盘绕程度高。在思想意识方面也有了新的变化，秦始皇嬴政被称为"祖龙"（《史记·秦始皇本纪》），汉高祖刘邦被称为"赤帝子"（《史记·高祖本纪》），龙形象与皇权紧密联系在一起。

汉武帝开疆拓土、凿通丝路，吸纳外来文化因素。龙如其时代，艺术上融汇东西，形象昂扬奔放、活泼自由，四象成形，乘龙升天较为普遍。汉代的龙翼较为流行，加装了山羊胡子般的髯和肘鬃，也出现了狮头形双角、单角的辟邪、麒麟等瑞兽。

里耶秦简记载了十二生肖，当时还没有龙，龙的位置是"虫"。"虫"是鳞虫之长。鳞虫主要指鳄鱼、蜥蜴、蛇等。汉代时十二生肖中"龙"最终取代了"虫"。十二生肖成为中国传统文化的重要内容。

有研究者认为，民俗"二龙戏珠"的"二龙"便是龙的阴阳二体，而阴阳二龙所戏的"珠"则是古代观象授时中东方苍龙七宿中的宿二（又称大火星或龙星）的原型。龙星在天为阳，自是星神，入地为阴，则化为社神。"二龙戏珠"实际表现的是对龙星或大火星的自然崇拜，汉代瓦当上的东方青龙正好驮着大火星，开启了"二龙戏珠"的先河。

青龙纹瓦当（闫西东门 138）

时　　代：汉
尺　　寸：直径 18.8 厘米
出土地点：陕西汉长安城南郊
现　藏　地：中国考古博物馆

Tile-end with Azure Loong Design
Han Dynasty
Diameter 18.8 cm
Excavated from south suburb of Chang'an City in Western Han Dynasty, Shaanxi Province
Chinese Archaeological Museum

　　出土于南郊礼制建筑。模制，宽边轮。中央为一乳钉，当面有一龙，屈身利爪，双目上扬。青龙纹瓦当与白虎纹瓦当、朱雀纹瓦当、玄武纹瓦当并称为"四神瓦当"。四神代表四个方位的星宿，具有辟邪的作用。

玉双龙佩（甬：329）

时　　代：西汉
尺　　寸：长 19.6、宽 6.2 厘米
出土地点：江苏徐州狮子山楚王墓
现 藏 地：徐州博物馆

Double Loong-shaped Jade Pendant
Western Han Dynasty
Length 19.6 cm, width 6.2 cm
Excavated from the Tomb of the King of Chu at Shizishan,
Xuzhou, Jiangsu Province
Xuzhou Museum

　　青白玉质，局部有沁色。透雕而成，主要纹样为盘曲对称的双龙，玉佩两端对称透雕反顾状龙首。龙身虬曲，饰有谷纹，龙身下有变形卷云纹。二龙相背而接，形如玉璜。河南信阳长台关楚墓和湖北江陵雨台山楚墓都出土过类似的玉佩。

玉龙形佩（W5∶14）

时　　代：西汉
尺　　寸：长22、宽7.8、厚0.2厘米
出土地点：江苏徐州狮子山楚王墓
现 藏 地：徐州博物馆

Loong-shaped Jade Pendant
Western Han Dynasty
Length 22 cm, width 7.8 cm, thickness 0.2 cm
Excavated from the Tomb of the King of Chu at Shizishan,
Xuzhou, Jiangsu Province
Xuzhou Museum

　　楚王玉枕上的装饰组件。青白色。龙首反顾，龙身呈横式多曲状，线条流畅而生动，龙尾内卷，龙爪锐利。这种龙形玉佩流行于春秋战国至西汉前期，西汉中期以后虽偶有发现，但已不再为主要玉佩类型了。"S"形龙身的线条流畅而不柔弱，具有西汉早期玉龙的典型风格。

玉龙形佩（W5：72）

时　　代：西汉
尺　　寸：高 17.2、宽 10.8、厚 0.6 厘米
出土地点：江苏徐州狮子山楚王墓
现 藏 地：徐州博物馆

Loong-shaped Jade Pendant
Western Han Dynasty
Height 17.2 cm, width 10.8 cm, thickness 0.6 cm
Excavated from the Tomb of the King of Chu at Shizishan, Xuzhou,
Jiangsu Province
Xuzhou Museum

　　狮子山楚王墓出土玉龙形佩较多，竖式 "S" 形龙佩是最为典型的一类。该龙形佩由新疆和田玉雕琢而成，莹润有玻璃光泽，局部有沁斑。造型为单体龙，以浅浮雕、透雕技法整体雕出。圆眼，张口，露齿，鬣毛向两边卷曲，前肢曲折，爪趾锐利，龙尾上卷平削，通体饰涡纹。眼睛下方有一钻孔，为佩戴时的系穿用孔，表明这件玉龙为配饰。

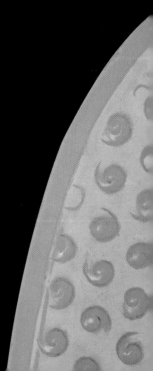

陶龙头把（1984YDT6M6：13）

时　代：汉
尺　寸：残长 8.1、宽 2.14 厘米
出土地点：河南偃师杏园汉墓
现 藏 地：中国考古博物馆

Pottery Handle in the Shape of Loong Head
Han Dynasty
Length 8.1 cm, width 2.14 cm
Excavated from Xingyuan tombs, Yanshi, Henan Province
Chinese Archaeological Museum

　　模制，龙首形，末端残存陶魁部分口沿，为陶魁手把。《说文·斗部》中解释："魁，羹斗也。"古人食用粥或肉汤等食物时，常使用魁作为盛放的器皿。目前最早的实物魁可追溯到西周时期，大多由漆木制成。至汉代，陶质魁开始广泛流行。

铜四神博局镜（LGM4：2）

时　　代：东汉
出土地点：云南罗平主山墓地M4
现　藏　地：罗平县博物馆

Bronze Mirror with Four Mythical Creatures Design
Eastern Han Dynasty
Excavated from No.4 Tomb of Guishan, Luoping,
Yunnan Province
Luoping County Museum

　　平缘，半球形钮，柿蒂形钮座。镜背主纹区饰博局纹，以四个圈状乳钉分为四区，分别饰青龙、白虎、朱雀和玄武，并搭配羽人、凤鸟等纹饰。龙呈奔走状，回首张口，长尾卷曲。此类铜镜流行于新莽时期至东汉前期，反映了汉武帝开西南夷后中原文化在当地的传播和发展。

281

（背景大字）南北朝 两晋 三国

【三国两晋南北朝】

　　三国两晋南北朝时期，龙的形象在延续汉代传统的同时，受佛教的影响也显露出来，比如有的龙上唇和鼻子模仿摩羯鱼的特点。北方的龙矫健敦实、蕴含张力，南方的龙丰盈修长、飘逸如仙。这时的龙多半是神龙，清俊超逸，一身傲骨，尽显魏晋风度。龙翼多呈飘动的火焰状，或称之为"肘鬃膊焰"。龙腿变细，小腿似包着鳞皮的鸟胫，更使它和兽体龙判然两途。北魏云冈石窟中的龙和河南邓州南朝彩色画像砖墓中的龙均可为代表。

山西大同云冈石窟第 12 窟（北魏时期）拱门上方龙形象

金龙形项饰（N2Z1M4：2）

时　　代：魏晋
尺　　寸：通长 128 厘米
出土地点：内蒙古达茂旗西河子
现 藏 地：乌兰察布市博物院

Loong-shaped Gold Necklace
Wei and Jin Dynasties
Length 128 cm
Excavated from Xihezi, Darhan Muminggan United Banner,
Inner Mongolia Autonomous Region
Ulanqab Municipal Museum

文明因交流而多彩，文明因互鉴而丰富。汉晋时期，中国龙的形象在欧亚大陆的交流和传播更为广泛和深入。此件金龙形项饰龙身用金丝编缀成绞索式管状空腔，两端龙头以金片卷制，龙角以金丝缠绕。这件混合了斯基泰、犍陀罗等诸种工艺手法，并带有佛教艺术色彩的首饰，在我国被称为"五兵佩"。"五兵佩"是一种较长的项饰，佩戴时多拖垂于胸前，与璎珞相似，其特点是在项链上缀有兵器模型，在魏晋时期流行。这件五兵佩饰有两盾、两戟和一钺，其上均有圆圈纹和鱼子纹，是西晋时期中外文化交流的有力见证。

《晋书·五行志》说："惠帝元康中，妇人之饰有五兵佩，又以金银琉璃之属，为斧钺戈戟，以当笄。"此记事出自干宝《搜神记》（《太平御览》卷三三九、六九二引），亦见《宋书·五行志》。

【隋】

　　隋代，河北赵县安济桥石栏板浮雕二龙对穿岩穴，非常精彩。龙在激流旋涡间穿游，隐去龙身的中段，开启宋代龙纹三段式隐身的艺术先河。

河北赵县隋代安济桥石栏板
（资料来源：《中国建筑艺术全集·桥梁、水利建筑》）

【 唐 】

唐代，龙多为行龙，或走或坐或飞，动静之中蕴含着力量和刚健，充分体现了盛唐气象。杜甫诗说："高帝子孙尽隆准，龙种自与常人殊。""云移雉尾开宫扇，日绕龙鳞识圣颜。"唐玄宗将他的生日八月初五定为千秋节，这一天皇帝赐群臣铜镜，王公以下亦献镜及承露囊。千秋节时颁赐和进奉之镜主要是带"千秋"铭文的盘龙镜。

河南偃师杏园唐墓出土的云龙纹铜镜
（资料来源：《偃师杏园唐墓》）

三彩龙柄壶（1985YDM1008：23）

时　　代：唐
尺　　寸：口径7.5、底径9.3、高34.9厘米
出土地点：河南偃师杏园唐墓
现 藏 地：中国考古博物馆

Tri-coloured Ewer with Loong-shaped Handle
Tang Dynasty
Mouth diameter 7.5 cm, foot diameter 9.3 cm, height 34.9 cm
Excavated from Xingyuan tombs, Yanshi, Henan Province
Chinese Archaeological Museum

小口卷唇，细颈圆肩，深腹平底。龙形柄细长，龙身置于肩部，龙嘴衔于壶唇缘。原应为双柄，一柄残失。肩以上施绿釉及黄褐色釉，腹下部无釉，露出坚硬的浅黄色胎。龙柄壶盛行于初唐和盛唐时期，多见于西安和洛阳地区。其龙纹造型显然是中国本土文化的产物。至于器型，一方面承袭了西晋以后鸡首壶的传统，另一方面则反映出罗马和波斯文化的影响，体现了多种文化因素的交融和互鉴。

陶生肖龙（1985YDM2731：2）

时　　代：唐
尺　　寸：宽6.5、高24.2厘米
出土地点：河南偃师杏园唐墓
现　藏　地：中国考古博物馆

Pottery Loong Figurine from Chinese Zodiac
Tang Dynasty
Width 6.5 cm, height 24.2 cm
Excavated from Xingyuan tombs, Yanshi, Henan Province
Chinese Archaeological Museum

　　龙首人身站立状，双手拱于胸前，身着交领宽袖袍，胸间束带，下裳长垂至地，脚下无托板。龙首无角，吻部前伸，头颈自然弯曲。

　　十二生肖在中国有着悠久的传承历史，与中国古代的干支纪年密切关联。云梦睡虎地出土的秦简证明，十二生肖的源头至少可上溯至战国时期。最早的十二生肖俑实物出现于北朝时期，隋唐时期发展至鼎盛。唐宋墓葬盛行包括十二生肖在内的各种神煞俑组合，或认为起辟邪压胜、祈求神灵庇佑之用，或认为与道教雷神相关。

　　偃师杏园唐墓群共出土十二生肖陶俑36件。此件生肖龙俑出自寿春霍丘县令郑琇及其妻卢氏合葬墓，生肖俑沿墓室四壁等距摆放，保存较好，是当时北方地区生肖俑的代表，也印证了《唐六典》等文献中关于随葬明器"四神十二时"的记载。

釉陶兽头（T405：7）

时　　代：唐
尺　　寸：长 43、宽 31.5、高 27 厘米
出土地点：黑龙江渤海上京城遗址
现 藏 地：中国考古博物馆

Glazed Pottery Beast Head
Tang Dynasty
Length 43 cm, width 31.5 cm, height 27 cm
Excavated from Shangjing City site, Bohai,
Heilongjiang Province
Chinese Archaeological Museum

建筑构件，出土于渤海上京城 1 号佛寺遗址正殿北部。兽首两眼圆睁，双眼皮，张口露齿，有犬齿和门齿，卷舌，有两竖耳，脑后可见竖鬃三条。形体较大，体内有铁条穿入。

兽头是中国古代屋顶瓦饰的重要种类，安装于屋脊的端头。有研究认为，兽头的前身是南北朝时期的浮雕状兽面砖，唐代逐渐演化成立体的兽首造型。这件兽头恰是这种转变的重要体现之一。

石螭首（QT31④：246）

时　代：唐
尺　寸：长 74、宽 29、高 21 厘米
出土地点：河南洛阳隋唐洛阳城上阳宫遗址
现 藏 地：中国考古博物馆

Stone Head of *Chi*
Tang Dynasty
Length 74 cm, width 29 cm, height 21 cm
Excavated from site of Sui-Tang period Shangyang
Palace of Luoyang City, Luoyang, Henan Province
Chinese Archaeological Museum

出土于隋唐洛阳城上阳宫园林遗址水池西侧的入水口，为整块青石精雕而成。螭首背脊有水槽，前端为龙首，水槽与龙口贯通。龙首张口卷鼻，獠牙外露，栩栩如生，为唐代石雕中的精品。上阳宫始建于唐高宗上元年间，是高宗、武则天时期重要的宫廷政治活动场所。螭首是建筑台基上围栏构件的组成部分，具有排水实用功能的同时，亦彰显了唐代皇室园林建筑的崇重规格和等级。

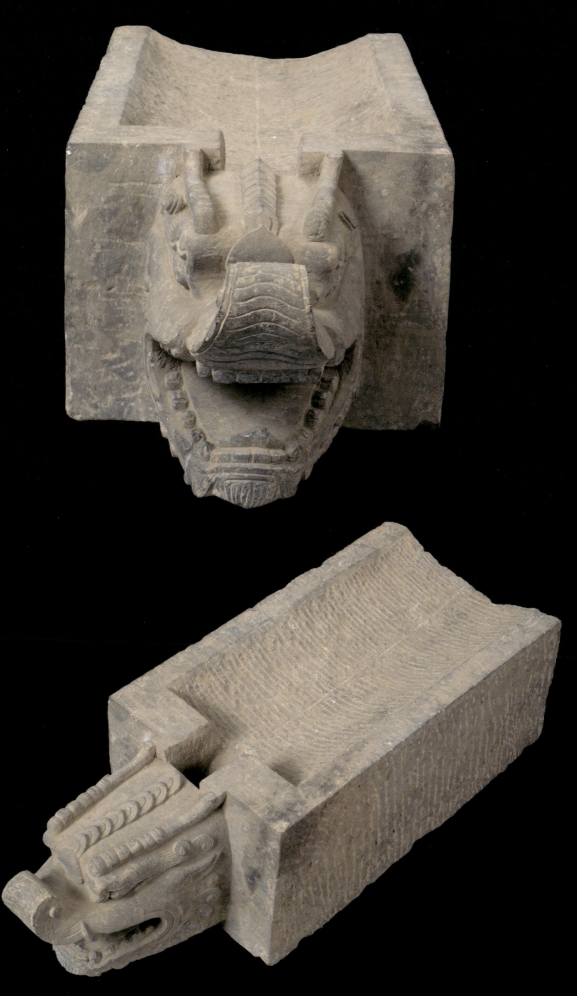

金质龙纹马鞍饰（2018DRXM1 主墓室扰土：717）

时　　代：唐
尺　　寸：残长 28.8、宽 9.5 厘米
出土地点：青海都兰热水墓群 2018 血渭一号墓
现 藏 地：青海省文物考古研究院

Gold Saddle Decoration with Loong Design
Tang Dynasty
Length 28.8 cm, width 9.5 cm
Excavated from 2018 Excavation of Xuewei Tomb No.1,
Reshui Tomb Cluster, Dulan, Qinghai Province
Qinghai Provincial Institute of Cultural Relics and
Archaeology

器身捶揲有多种动植物纹样，其中右侧主体为一立龙。龙体修长，头部有耳、发，一侧龙首上有单叉状角，龙口咧开，上唇外翻，口吐云气，四肢上下而舞，似为三爪，前肢处生翼，根部似涡纹状。根据树木年轮测定和出土印章的释读，2018 血渭一号墓的墓主可能是吐蕃治下的吐谷浑王莫贺吐浑可汗。该墓葬是热水墓群乃至青藏高原地区发现的布局最完整、结构最清晰、形制最复杂的高等级墓葬之一。这件精美的鞍饰既是吐谷浑王陵等级的标志，亦是丝绸之路青海道的见证。

铜八卦生肖镜

时　　代：晚唐五代
尺　　寸：边长14、厚0.3厘米
出土地点：江苏扬州润扬北路西延工地
现　藏　地：扬州市文物考古研究所

Bronze Mirror with the Eight Diagrams and Chinese Zodiac Design
Late Tang Dynasty and Five Dynasties
Side length 14 cm, thickness 0.3 cm
Excavated from construction site of Runyang North Road, Yangzhou, Jiangsu Province
Yangzhou Municipal Institute of Cultural Relics and Archaeology

　　方形，桥形钮。内区为一周八卦符号。外区为十二生肖，生肖绕镜心按顺时针方向排列。镜四角为云纹。整体黑灰色，部分锈蚀。这类八卦镜具有浓厚的道教因素，除了一般铜镜都具有的映面照容的实用功能，其装饰纹样还具有丰富的社会文化价值，古人相信其有预示吉凶、避邪鉴物的功效。

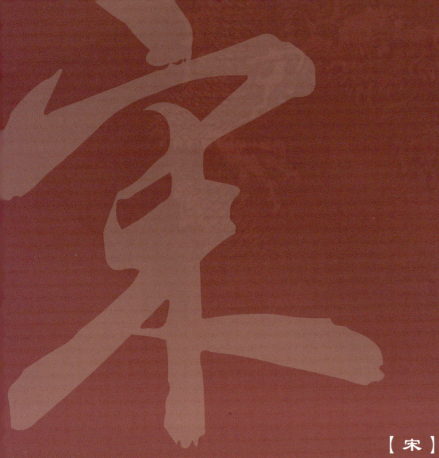

【宋】

　　宋代，龙的形象基本定型，成为后世比较稳定的模仿样式。南宋《尔雅翼》记载龙"角似鹿，头似驼，眼似兔，颈似蛇，腹似蜃，鳞似鱼，爪似鹰，掌似虎，耳似牛"。南宋陈容的《九龙图》充分体现了宋代对龙三停九似的定义和表现手法。

　　辽、金和西夏基本沿用唐代龙的形象。

南宋陈容的《九龙图》（局部）

陶龙形脊饰（DT46④：87）

时　　代：北宋
尺　　寸：总长60、宽20、高28厘米
出土地点：河南洛阳东城宋园遗址
现 藏 地：中国考古博物馆

Pottery Roof Decoration in the Shape of Loong
Northern Song Dynasty
Length 60 cm, width 20 cm, height 28 cm
Excavated from site of Songyuan in eastern palace of Luoyang,
Henan Province
Chinese Archaeological Museum

　　分前后两部分。前端为凸出的龙首，额心阴刻"王"字；后端为一板瓦状底座。这类脊饰即《营造法式》中提及的脊饰"兽头"。相较唐代的早期兽头，此时龙首造型更显细长纤秀，形象华丽。兽头在高规格建筑中使用较普遍，但遗址中所见者往往是建筑倒塌后形成的破碎残块。此件标本历经千年仍保存完整，殊为难得，是建筑考古和城市考古研究中重要的标型器。

鎏金盘龙镜

时　　代：辽
尺　　寸：直径28、厚1厘米
出土地点：内蒙古赤峰阿鲁科尔沁旗耶律羽之墓
现　藏　地：内蒙古自治区文物考古研究院

Gilded-gold Bronze Mirror with Loong Design
Liao Dynasty
Diameter 28 cm, thickness 1 cm
Excavated from Tomb of Yelvyuzhi, Ar Horqin Banner,
Chifeng, Inner Mongolia Autonomous Region
Inner Mongolia Institute of Cultural Relics and Archaeology

圆钮，镜背模铸一盘龙，龙首昂起，双角耸立，张口吐舌，与中央圆钮形成龙口衔珠之势。背鳍、腹甲、鳞片、肘毛刻画清晰。龙四肢四爪雄健有力，后腿与龙尾缠绕，通体饰鱼鳞纹。耶律羽之是辽初的皇室重戚，墓葬极尽奢华，这件鎏金盘龙镜既是墓主身份的象征，亦是辽承唐风的体现。

【元】

　　元代统治者严格限定了龙的使用标准，双角五爪龙成为皇权的象征。这一时期的龙身形较细长，原来长着象征性羽翼的位置，已被宛曲多叉的火焰纹替代，有的龙尾添上尾鳍。在形象的处理上，行龙、立龙、升龙、降龙无不挥洒自如。元代瓷器上的龙纹完美地展现了此时期的龙形象。

青花龙纹高足杯

时　　代：元

尺　　寸：杯高 10.6、口径 12.2、底径 3.9 厘米

出土地点：内蒙古赤峰林西县大营子乡前地村

现 藏 地：林西博物馆

Blue and White Porcelain Stem Cup with Loong Design
Yuan Dynasty
Height 10.6 cm, mouth diameter 12.2 cm, foot diameter 3.9 cm
Excavated from Qiandi Village, Dayingzi Town, Linxi County,
Chifeng, Inner Mongolia Autonomous Region
Linxi Museum

　　杯口外侈，深腹，空心喇叭形竹节纹高圈足。口沿内饰青花草叶纹一周，内壁饰素纹飞龙，杯内底饰青花火焰纹；杯外壁饰青花单龙云纹，细颈，三爪，头尾间饰火焰纹，尾部饰一灵芝状云朵纹。高足杯既可作为酒器，亦可用于供奉祭祀，是元代青花瓷最具代表性的器型之一。

青花龙纹盘

时　　代：元
尺　　寸：高 4.1、口径 15.9、底径 5.2 厘米
出土地点：内蒙古赤峰林西县大营子乡前地村
现 藏 地：林西博物馆

Blue and White Porcelain Plate with Loong Design
Yuan Dynasty
Height 4.1 cm, mouth diameter 15.9 cm, foot diameter 5.2 cm
Excavated from Qiandi Village, Dayingzi Town, Linxi County,
Chifeng, Inner Mongolia Autonomous Region
Linxi Museum

盘圆唇，侈口，弧腹，圈足微外撇。盘内壁腹部饰两道旋纹，旋纹间饰缠枝花纹。盘内底饰团龙纹，龙纹身躯细长如蛇，龙头呈扁长形，双角，张口露齿，细长颈，四肢细瘦，筋腱凹凸，三爪分张有力，肘毛、尾鬃呈火焰状。盘外壁口沿饰一道旋纹，腹壁饰两道旋纹，旋纹间饰缠枝葵花纹。

白地黑花龙凤纹瓷扁壶（YMF2：3）

时　　代：元
尺　　寸：高 32.6、宽 31 厘米
出土地点：北京元大都遗址
现 藏 地：中国考古博物馆

White Glazed Porcelain Flat Flask with Loong and Phoenix Design
Yuan Dynasty
Height 32.6 cm, width 31 cm
Excavated from site of Yuandadu, Beijing
Chinese Archaeological Museum

　　扁方形，小口，腹部微鼓，肩部有四系，平底。腹部两面在白地上用黑彩分别绘出龙、凤纹，并刻划出鳞片和羽毛，侧面饰卷草纹。黑白双色对比强烈，龙凤纹样线条流畅。白地黑花是宋元时期中原北方地区最流行的瓷器品种之一。这件扁壶的造型又兼具草原民族特征，或认为与皮囊壶有关。此壶出自元朝最重要的都城——元大都遗址，是当时民族文化交融的重要物质载体。

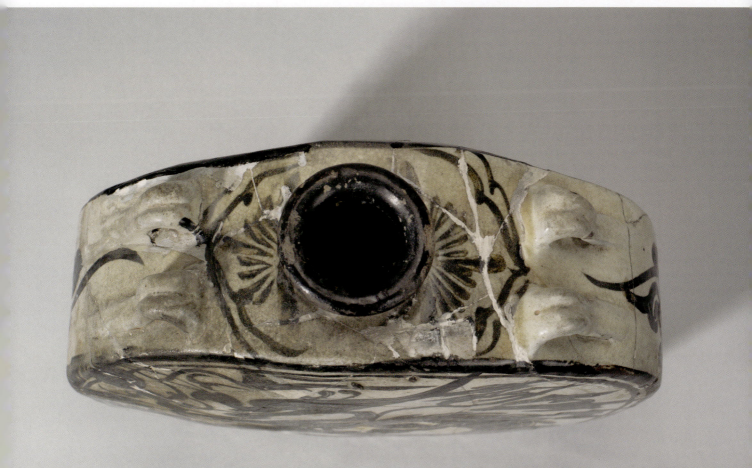

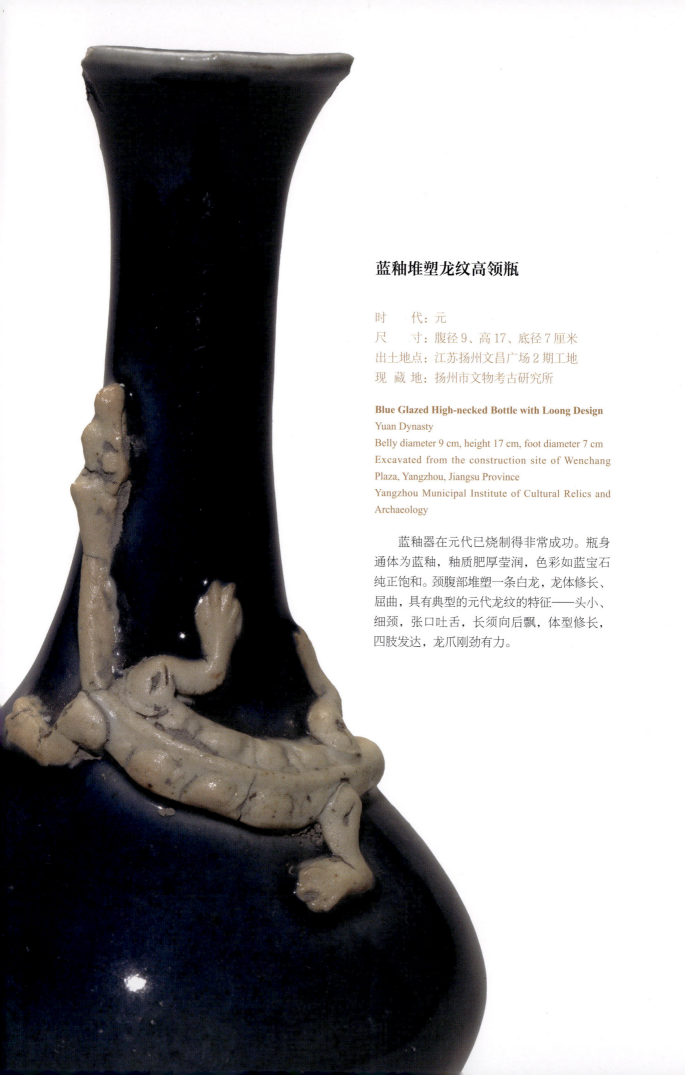

蓝釉堆塑龙纹高领瓶

时　　代：元
尺　　寸：腹径 9、高 17、底径 7 厘米
出土地点：江苏扬州文昌广场 2 期工地
现 藏 地：扬州市文物考古研究所

Blue Glazed High-necked Bottle with Loong Design
Yuan Dynasty
Belly diameter 9 cm, height 17 cm, foot diameter 7 cm
Excavated from the construction site of Wenchang
Plaza, Yangzhou, Jiangsu Province
Yangzhou Municipal Institute of Cultural Relics and
Archaeology

　　蓝釉器在元代已烧制得非常成功。瓶身通体为蓝釉，釉质肥厚莹润，色彩如蓝宝石纯正饱和。颈腹部堆塑一条白龙，龙体修长、屈曲，具有典型的元代龙纹的特征——头小、细颈，张口吐舌，长须向后飘，体型修长，四肢发达，龙爪刚劲有力。

【明清】

　　明代编撰了龙生九子的故事，为早已存在的各类龙形神兽正名并赋予其龙种的身份。明代中晚期出现的正面脸的正龙纹成为皇家御用的图案。清代继续沿用这种徽章式的正龙纹。

　　明弘治年间，明孝宗朱祐樘曾命宦官问询李东阳龙生九子的名目，李东阳请教了翰林院编修罗玘、吏部员外郎刘绩等人，又经过多方考证，最终给出的答案是："龙生九子不成龙，各有所好：囚牛，龙种，平生好音乐，今胡琴头上刻兽是其遗像；睚眦，平生好杀，今刀柄上龙吞口是其遗像；嘲风，平生好险，今殿角走兽是其遗像；蒲牢，平生好鸣，今钟上兽纽是其遗像；狻猊，平生好坐，今佛座狮子是其遗像；霸下，平生好负重，今碑座兽是其遗像；狴犴，平生好讼，今狱门上狮子头是其遗像；赑屃，平生好文，今碑两旁龙是其遗像；蚩吻，平生好吞，今殿脊兽头是其遗像。"
（资料来源：《怀麓堂集》）

龙首青釉瓷水注

时　　代：明
尺　　寸：腹径 10、底径 3—3.3、高 6.5 厘米
出土地点：河南郑州黄岗寺村明代墓葬
现　藏　地：郑州市文物考古研究院

Celadon Water Dropper with Loong-head Design
Ming Dynasty
Belly diameter 10 cm, foot diameter 3-3.3 cm, height 6.5 cm
Excavated from Ming Dynasty Tomb, Huanggangsi Village,
Zhengzhou, Henan Province
Zhengzhou Municipal Institute of Archaeology

　　瓷壶体小，白胎，腹部以上施黄釉，腹部以下
露胎。口隐于盖下，弧肩，鼓腹，下腹斜收，假圈足，
平底。体侧置一龙首状短流，肩部设三环式錾手，
錾手下为双层覆莲式盖，盖顶圆珠钮，流、盖、錾
连做。肩、腹部有凹弦纹两周。水注是一种形似注
壶的文房用具，又称砚滴，起贮水之用，与砚合用。

光绪元宝

时　　代：清
尺　　寸：直径 3.9、厚 0.3 厘米
出土地点：江苏扬州供电局宿舍
现 藏 地：扬州市文物考古研究所

Guangxu Ingot
Qing Dynasty
Diameter 3.9 cm, thickness 0.3 cm
Excavated from the dormitory of Jiangsu
Yangzhou Power Supply Company
Yangzhou Municipal Institute of Cultural
Relics and Archaeology

　　银质，正面中央为满汉双语的"光绪元宝"四字，其上镌"北洋造"，下镌"库平七钱二分"。背面中心为蟠龙，龙直视前方，身躯扭动。前肢高举在头部两侧；后肢露出一只，伸向体侧；均为五爪。龙身周围环绕云纹。银币上下方分别印"29th YEAR OF KUANG HSU"和"PEI YANG"。币面部分锈蚀。光绪元宝是清末吸收西方工艺，开展币制改革的重要产物。

天行健，君子以自强不息。时至今日，作为中华民族的图腾和中华文化的标志性符号，龙不仅成为中国人民喜爱的吉祥物，以舞龙为主题的节庆活动也在世界范围内得到广泛传播，成为向世界讲好中国故事的重要媒介。

龙·中华民族的图腾

——中国八千年龙文化精品文物展

前言

习近平总书记在甲辰龙年春节团拜会的重要讲话中指出，龙是中华民族的图腾，具有刚健威武的雄姿、勇猛无畏的气概、福泽四海的情怀、强大无比的力量。甲辰龙年，让我们从一件件考古发掘出土的精美文物中探寻博大精深、绵延至今的中国龙文化！

二里头遗址绿松石龙形器

《诗·周颂·载见》："载见辟王，曰求厥章。龙旂阳阳，和铃央央。鞗革有鸧，休有烈光。"

金文"展"字

结　语

　　龙的起源、发展和演变充分体现了中华文明突出的连续性、创新性、统一性、包容性、和平性。

　　龙出东方，从新石器时代满天星斗的各地原始文化中以图腾的形式孕育而生，随着多元一体的重瓣花朵式史前社会发展而融汇创新；龙行天下，在中原广域王权国家形成和发展过程中逐渐成形，成为中华文明中最重要的文化基因；龙泽四海，其形象及精神实质自秦汉一统一直延续至今，充满了"日日新"的勃勃生机和生命力。

　　习近平总书记在甲辰龙年春节团拜会的重要讲话中指出，龙"既象征着五千年来中华民族自强不息、奋斗进取的精神血脉，更承载着新时代新征程亿万中华儿女推进强国建设、民族复兴伟业的坚定意志和美好愿望"。历久更新的中华龙必将鼓舞中华儿女在新时代从胜利走向胜利，敦厚吉祥的中华龙必将为世界贡献更多的美好和福泽。

参考文献

史料文献

（汉）司马迁撰：《史记》，中华书局，1959年。

（汉）班固撰：《汉书》，中华书局，1962年。

（汉）郑玄笺，（唐）孔颖达疏：《毛诗注疏》，上海古籍出版社，2013年。

（汉）许慎撰，（清）段玉裁注：《说文解字注》，上海古籍出版社，1988年。

（魏）王弼、（晋）韩康伯注，（唐）孔颖达疏：《周易正义》，上海古籍出版社，1990年。

（西晋）陈寿撰：《三国志》，中华书局，1982年。

（东晋）干宝撰，李剑国辑校：《搜神记辑校》，中华书局，2019年。

（南朝宋）范晔撰：《后汉书》，中华书局，1965年。

（南朝梁）沈约撰：《宋书》，中华书局，1974年。

（南朝梁）萧子显撰：《南齐书》，中华书局，1972年。

（北齐）魏收撰：《魏书》，中华书局，1974年。

（唐）房玄龄等撰：《晋书》，中华书局，1974年。

（唐）姚思廉撰：《梁书》，中华书局，1973年。

（唐）姚思廉撰：《陈书》，中华书局，1972年。

（唐）李百药撰：《北齐书》，中华书局，1972年。

（唐）令狐德棻等撰：《周书》，中华书局，1971年。

（唐）李延寿撰：《南史》，中华书局，1975年。

（唐）李延寿撰：《北史》，中华书局，1974年。

（唐）魏徵、（唐）令狐德棻撰：《隋书》，中华书局，1973年。

（唐）李林甫等撰，陈仲夫点校：《唐六典》，中华书局，1992年。

（唐）李吉甫撰，贺次君点校：《元和郡县图志》，中华书局，1983年。

（唐）杜甫著，（清）仇兆鳌注：《杜诗详注》，中华书局，1979年。

（唐）刘禹锡撰，卞孝萱校订：《刘禹锡集》，中华书局，1990年。

（唐）徐坚等著：《初学记》，中华书局，2004年。

（后晋）刘昫等撰：《旧唐书》，中华书局，1975年。

（宋）欧阳修、（宋）宋祁撰：《新唐书》，中华书局，1975年。

（宋）王溥撰：《唐会要》，中华书局，1960年。

（宋）司马光编著：《资治通鉴》，中华书局，1956年。

（宋）李昉等撰：《太平御览》，中华书局，1960年。

（宋）罗愿撰，石云孙校点：《尔雅翼》，黄山书社，2013年。

（元）脱脱等撰：《宋史》，中华书局，1985年。

（明）宋濂等撰：《元史》，中华书局，1976年。

（明）李东阳撰：《怀麓堂集》，上海古籍出版社，1991年。

（清）徐松辑：《宋会要辑稿》，上海古籍出版社，2014年。

（清）张廷玉等撰：《明史》，中华书局，1974年。

（清）赵尔巽等撰：《清史稿》，中华书局，1977年。

（清）阮元校刻：《十三经注疏（清嘉庆刊本）》，中华书局，2009年。

刘庆柱辑注：《三秦记辑注·关中记辑注》，三秦出版社，2006年。

专著

河南省文化局文物工作队编：《邓县彩色画象砖墓》，文物出版社，1958年。

中国科学院考古研究所编辑：《长安张家坡西周铜器群》，文物出版社，1965年。

湖南省博物馆、中国科学院考古研究所编：《长沙马王堆一号汉墓》，文物出版社，1973年。

中国社会科学院考古研究所编辑：《殷墟妇好墓》，文物出版社，1980年。

中国社会科学院考古研究所编著：《小屯南地甲骨》，中华书局，1983年。

中国社会科学院考古研究所编著：《六顶山与渤海镇——唐代渤海国的贵族墓地与都城遗址》，中国大百科全书出版社，1997年。

冯先铭主编：《中国古陶瓷图典》，文物出版社，1998年。

中国社会科学院考古研究所编著：《偃师二里头

1959年—1978年考古发掘报告》，中国大百科全书出版社，1999年。

四川省文物考古研究所编：《三星堆祭祀坑》，文物出版社，1999年。

中国社会科学院考古研究所编著：《张家坡西周墓地》，中国大百科全书出版社，1999年。

安徽省文物考古研究所编：《凌家滩玉器》，文物出版社，2000年。

中国社会科学院考古研究所编著：《偃师杏园唐墓》，科学出版社，2001年。

河南省商丘文物管理委员会、河南省文物考古研究所、河南省永城市文物管理委员会编著：《芒砀山西汉梁王墓地》，文物出版社，2001年。

潘洪萱主编：《中国建筑艺术全集·桥梁、水利建筑》，中国建筑工业出版社，2001年。

谭维四：《曾侯乙墓》，文物出版社，2001年。

浙江省文物考古研究所编著：《瑶山》，文物出版社，2003年。

中国社会科学院考古研究所编著：《西汉礼制建筑遗址》，文物出版社，2003年。

中国社会科学院考古研究所编著：《安阳小屯》，世界图书出版公司北京公司，2004年。

中国社会科学院考古研究所编著：《滕州前掌大墓地》，文物出版社，2005年。

安徽省文物考古研究所编著：《凌家滩——田野考古发掘报告之一》，文物出版社，2006年。

中国社会科学院考古研究所编著：《安阳殷墟花园庄东地商代墓葬》，科学出版社，2007年。

中国社会科学院考古研究所编：《张家坡西周玉器》，文物出版社，2007年。

北京大学震旦古代文明研究中心、郑州市文物考古研究院：《新密新砦——1999—2000年田野考古发掘报告》，文物出版社，2008年。

朱凤瀚：《中国青铜器综论》，上海古籍出版社，2009年。

王世仁主编：《中国美术全集·建筑（四）》，黄山书社，2010年。

中国社会科学院考古研究所编著：《安阳殷墟小屯建筑遗存》，文物出版社，2010年。

辽宁省文物考古研究所编著：《查海：新石器时代聚落遗址发掘报告》，文物出版社，2012年。

辽宁省文物考古研究所编著：《牛河梁——红山文化遗址发掘报告（1983—2003年度）》，文物出版社，2012年。

河南省文物考古研究所、濮阳市文物保护管理所编：《濮阳西水坡》，中州古籍出版社，2012年。

张光直：《考古学专题六讲》，生活·读书·新知三联书店，2013年。

中国社会科学院考古研究所编著：《二里头（1999—2006）》，文物出版社，2014年。

中国社会科学院考古研究所编著：《隋唐洛阳城：1959—2001年考古发掘报告》，文物出版社，2014年。

中国社会科学院考古研究所、山西省临汾市文物局编著：《襄汾陶寺——1978—1985年考古发掘报告》，文物出版社，2015年。

湖南省博物馆编：《长沙马王堆汉墓陈列》，中华书局，2017年。

冯时：《文明以止：上古的天文、思想与制度》，中国社会科学出版社，2018年。

葛明宇：《狮子山西汉楚王陵墓考古研究》，河北美术出版社，2018年。

中国社会科学院考古研究所编著：《安阳殷墟孝民屯》（三）《殷商遗存·铸铜遗物》，文物出版社，2020年。

中国社会科学院考古研究所、北京市文物管理处编著：《元大都——1964—1974年考古报告》，文物出版社，2024年。

简报、论文

安阳亦工亦农文物考古短训班、中国科学院考古研究所安阳发掘队：《安阳殷墟奴隶祭祀坑的发掘》，《考古》1977年第1期。

中国社会科学院考古研究所安阳工作队：《1969—1977年殷墟西区墓葬发掘报告》，《考古学报》1979年第1期。

中国社会科学院考古研究所安阳工作队：《安阳小屯村北的两座殷代墓》，《考古学报》1981年第4期。

陆思贤、陈棠栋：《达茂旗出土古代北方民族金龙等贵重文物》，《内蒙古社会科学》1983年第4期。

中国社会科学院考古研究所内蒙古工作队：《内蒙古敖汉旗小山遗址》，《考古》1987年第6期。

李学勤：《西水坡"龙虎墓"与四象的起源》，《中国社会科学院研究生院学报》1988年第5期。

濮阳西水坡遗址考古队：《1988年河南濮阳西水坡遗址发掘简报》，《考古》1989年第12期。

冯时：《河南濮阳西水坡45号墓的天文学研究》，《文物》1990年第3期。

内蒙古文物考古研究所、赤峰市博物馆、阿鲁科尔沁旗文物管理所：《辽耶律羽之墓发掘简报》，《文物》1996年第1期。

何星亮：《河南濮阳仰韶文化蚌壳龙的象征意义》，《中原文物》1998年第2期。

北京大学考古学系、浙江省文物考古研究所、日本上智大学联合考古队：《浙江桐乡普安桥遗址发掘简报》，《文物》1998年第4期。

狮子山楚王陵考古发掘队：《徐州狮子山西汉楚王陵发掘简报》，《文物》1998年第8期。

韦正、李虎仁、邹厚本：《江苏徐州市狮子山西汉墓的发掘与收获》，《考古》1998年第8期。

张敬国：《含山凌家滩遗址第三次考古发掘主要收获》，《东南文化》1999年第5期。

安徽省文物考古研究所、含山县文物管理所：《安徽含山县凌家滩遗址第三次发掘简报》，《考古》1999年第11期。

中国社会科学院考古研究所内蒙古第一工作队：《内蒙古赤峰市兴隆沟聚落遗址2002—2003年的发掘》，《考古》2004年第7期。

朱乃诚：《二里头文化"龙"遗存研究》，《中原文物》2006年第4期。

赵德云：《从鸡头壶到龙柄壶的发展——兼析外来文化因素在这一过程中的作用》，《考古与文物》2007年第1期。

安徽省文物考古研究所：《安徽含山县凌家滩遗址第五次发掘的新发现》，《考古》2008年第3期。

荆州博物馆：《湖北荆州院墙湾一号楚墓》，《文物》2008年第4期。

郑州市文物考古研究院：《郑州黄岗寺明墓发掘简报》，《东方博物》2009年第2期。

蔡庆良：《商、西周玉器风格比较》，《紫禁城》2010年第3、4期。

李宸：《大酋长之墓——含山凌家滩07M23墓文化内涵试析》，《文物天地》2015年第4期。

方向明：《良渚玉器神人兽面像的真相》，《大众考古》2015年第6期。

沈丽华：《建筑基址出土螭首考古学初探》，《考古、艺术与历史——杨泓先生八秩华诞纪念文集》，文物出版社，2018年。

凌家滩遗址考古队：《安徽含山县凌家滩遗址新石器时代墓葬的清理》，《考古》2020年第11期。

武松、冯恩学：《浅析渤海的脊头瓦和兽头》，《考古》2020年第12期。

朱乃诚：《商代玉龙研究》，《文博学刊》2021年第3期。

凌家滩遗址考古队：《安徽含山县凌家滩遗址第四次发掘简报》，《东南文化》2021年第5期。

中国社会科学院考古研究所、青海省文物考古研究所：《青海都兰县热水墓群2018血渭一号墓》，《考古》2021年第8期。

何驽：《蟠龙根脉——中华精神"图腾"的面世》，《十件文物里的中国故事》，中国社会科学出版社，2022年。

安徽省文物考古研究所、含山县凌家滩遗址管理处：《安徽含山凌家滩遗址考古取得重大收获》，《中国文物报》2022年12月8日，第5版。

浙江省文物考古研究所：《杭州市余杭区官井头遗址良渚文化遗存》，《考古》2023年第1期。

高江涛：《试析陶寺遗址2022JXTIJ1出土动物形刻划纹饰》，《考古与文物》2024年第5期。

浙江省文物考古研究所、杭州市良渚遗址管理区管理委员会：《杭州市余杭区北村遗址北村南地点2020—2021年良渚文化遗存发掘简报》，《考古》2024年第6期。

后 记

在中华大地波澜壮阔的历史长河中，龙作为中华文明独一无二的精神标识，蜿蜒游弋了8000年的时光。岁月流转中，它记录了中华民族风雨兼程、自强不息的奋斗篇章，承载了中华儿女对强国建设的坚定期许、对民族复兴的深情渴盼。

甲辰龙年，习近平总书记在春节团拜会上的重要讲话为文化建设工作指明了方向。春节刚过，中国考古博物馆各位同人在院党组的部署下以满腔热情投入此次展览的筹备工作，积极响应党中央的号召，力求阐释好、呈现好龙文化的精神内涵，赓续中华文脉，传承发展中华优秀传统文化。

展陈理念是展览的核心与灵魂。筹备初期，中国社会科学院院长、党组书记，中国历史研究院院长、党委书记高翔同志精心选定"龙·中华民族的图腾"作为特展主题，并多次亲临现场悉心指导。高翔同志指出，展览不仅要展示精品文物，更要强化文献及科技手段的支撑，力求兼具学术性与观赏性。这一理念主线，始终指导贯穿着展览筹备的全过程。

在展览筹备期间，中国考古博物馆的全体同人和中国历史研究院考古研究所的专家们秉持着严谨专业的态度，高效完成了诸多艰巨任务，倾力为观众打造出集文化深度与科技魅力于一体、全方位立体式展现龙文化精髓的高品质文化盛宴。该展览的成功是在院党组、历史院党委领导下团结协作的集体智慧结晶，体现了中国历史研究院蓬勃向上、求真务实的工作氛围和锐意进取、勇于开拓的工作作风。

此次展览由中国历史研究院主办，中国历史研究院考古研究所和中国考古博物馆承办，在全国23家考古文博单位的大力支持下，来自全国各地的百余件精品龙文物跨越山海，齐聚一堂，共同讲述中华龙文化的悠久历史与深刻内涵。

本次展品均系科学考古发掘所获，用考古发掘出土的龙文化主题文物，实证了8000年中国龙文化，充分体现了中华文明的连续性、创新性、统一性、包容性、和平性，是构建中华文明标识体系的一次有益实践。该展览得到了媒体的广泛关注和社会各界的好评，《人民日报》、新华社及中央广播电视总台《新闻联播》《焦点访谈》等栏目对本次展览纷纷进行了报道。

龙，是中华民族的图腾，是中华儿女的情感纽带，是中华文明多元一体的重要象征，寄托着九州升平、海晏河清、物阜民丰、日月昭明的美好愿景。希望通过这本展览图录，能让您领略中国龙文化的魅力和风采。

中国考古博物馆

2025 年 1 月 5 日

龙腾盛世　龙韵华章　龙跃甲辰　龙踞华夏　龙马精神　龙吟九州　有龙则灵　龙语华夏　精神

龙吟九州　龙腾盛世　龙韵华章　龙腾盛世　龙马精神　龙踞华夏　龙吟九州

龙腾　龙吟九州　龙韵华章　龙马精神　有龙则灵　龙语华夏　龙吟九州　龙韵华章

龙彰华章　龙跃甲辰　龙马精神

图书在版编目（CIP）数据

龙：中华民族的图腾：中国八千年龙文化文物精品 /
中国历史研究院编 . -- 北京：社会科学文献出版社，
2025.4. -- ISBN 978-7-5228-4175-5

Ⅰ . B933；K870.2

中国国家版本馆 CIP 数据核字第 2024M6441S 号

龙：中华民族的图腾——中国八千年龙文化文物精品

编　　者 / 中国历史研究院

出 版 人 / 冀祥德
组稿编辑 / 郑庆寰
责任编辑 / 赵　晨　郑彦宁
责任印制 / 王钠鑫

出　　版 / 社会科学文献出版社·历史学分社（010）59367256
　　　　　　地址：北京市北三环中路甲29号院华龙大厦　邮编：100029
　　　　　　网址：www.ssap.com.cn
发　　行 / 社会科学文献出版社（010）59367028
印　　装 / 南京爱德印刷有限公司

规　　格 / 开　本：889mm×1194mm　1/16
　　　　　　印　张：21.5　字　数：180 千字
版　　次 / 2025年4月第1版　2025年4月第1次印刷
书　　号 / ISBN 978-7-5228-4175-5
定　　价 / 398.00元